KINGDOM KEYS for KINGDOM KIDS

WORKBOOK

Walking in Kingdom Power

Jeanne Metcalf

1st Edition 2014
2nd Edition 2015
3rd Edition 2023

International Copyright © 2023
Cëgullah Publishing
www.cegullahpublishing.ca
All rights reserved.

ISBN # Textbook: 978-1-926489-91-9
ISBN # Workbook: 978-1-926489-92-6

Cover photo © iStock # 13968191345 (2023)
Cover design by Jeanne Metcalf.

TO STUDENTS IN THE DEGREE PROGRAM

This workbook, like its accompanying textbook, holds 2 Courses: **COURSE 205 & 301.**

1. **Course 205 includes Section 1 & Section 2.**
   When finished, before moving on, be sure you complete the following:
   - Submit the reports at the end of Section 2.
   - Write the exam at the end of Section 2.
     - You must have 69% Grade to receive the credit hours.
     - You must have 75% Grade to continue to the next course.

NOTE: This course is worth 6 credits towards your degree.

2. **Course 301 is Section 3.**
   When finished, be sure you complete the following:
   - Submit the reports at the end of Section 3.
   - Write the exam at the end of Section 3.
     - You must have 69% Grade to receive the credit hours.
     - You must have 75% Grade to continue to the next course.

NOTE: This course is worth 6 credits towards your degree

COURSE GRADING

This Grading applies to Courses 302 and 303, entitled, Kingdom Keys for Kingdom Kids

SPECIFICS OF DEGREE GRADING	%
Online Course Audio Completion Acknowledgement...............	7
Course Completion Acknowledgement.............................	2
Workbook Completion Acknowledgement.........................	5
Workbook Chapter Reviews	18
Section Review Form..	12
Personal Testimony of your spiritual benefit from the course......	8
All of the above must be submitted before scheduling the final exam	52
Online Course Final Exam...	48
TOTAL	100
Passing Grade to receive credits.......................................	69
NOTE: Grade to continue taking courses for your degree	75

TO UNACCREDITED STUDENTS:

If you are studying unaccredited, we invite you to do all the exercises in the workbook, however, your study does not require the submission of reports or exams. Therefore, please overlook the messages regarding Course numbers, and information on the requirements at each section end. Simply move on to the next section.

We pray that as you do your homework, and perhaps, review your answers with others, that your roots in God will go down deep as you unravel the truths of the scriptures.

May God richly bless you.

TO ALL STUDENTS:

ALWAYS BEGIN EVERY COURSE WITH THE WORKBOOK!

Every course that we at Cegullah Publishing & Apologetics Academy designs, we write to present the student with an inductive style environment. Thus, students

Have opportunity for learning scriptures, first, on their own before we teach them. We do this because we believe every person who desires to learn God's Word can do so by prayerfully reading scriptures, by seeking the Holy Spirit for insight, and then, by reading the accompanying textbook to help keep the student on the right track. So, unless otherwise advised within the workbook, keep the textbook closed and only open after finishing that chapter.

HOW TO SPIRITUALLY BEGIN EVERY LESSON

Step # 1:   **IMPORTANT:**
Before you begin your study, take some time with YeHoVaH to prepare your heart to receive whatever He wishes to share with you. Do this every time you approach the workbook or read the textbook. In this way, you will make this time a deeply personal time of fellowship between you and your Heavenly Father, YeHoVaH!

A NOTE FROM THE AUTHOR

Many years ago, in an effort to better understand Income Tax, I took a course on how to prepare personal returns. At that time, the teacher made a blatant statement giving his listening audience a key to success: "Learn to read," he said, "follow the instructions and you will do well." He went on to explain that from his experience, students often skimmed the contents of the page, and thus, overlooked the steps giving them the simple instructions.

As a result, some students gave up preparing income tax, considering the job and its detailed entries, overwhelming. Other students, in a hurry to make money by doing returns, rushed with the forms, and inevitably missed entries or deductions. These made too many errors, which resulted in too much time spent going back over the forms to fix the problems.

As the teacher continued his talk, he went on to say he knew the key to success in income tax preparation. He said, "it rests in one's ability to *read the text and do what it says*".

This advice works well in the study of scripture, too.

DOING THE WORKBOOK

In this workbook, you will find many scriptures. Following the scripture, you will discover several questions about that scripture passage. Each question has a purpose. That purpose is to help you gain an understanding of the text. The secret to understanding the text rests in your ability to literally, *hear*[1] the words of the text. Therefore, as you answer the questions, use as much wording from the scripture as possible. ***Please do not add your opinion or even what you have been taught earlier about that passage.*** Approach each passage fresh.

---

[1] This is one reason why the Jews always read the text out loud.

Simply answer the questions using the wording of the scripture under study[2]. Why this may seem a redundant process, in the long run, it helps you learn.

HOW TO ANSWER FROM THE TEXT

John 14:6	
Jesus saith unto him, I am the way, the truth, and the life: no man cometh unto the Father, but by me.	
Question	Who is speaking in verse 6?
Answer	**Yeshua (Jesus)**
Question	What 3 things did Yeshua say about Himself?
Answer	**I am the way, the truth, and the life.**
Question	Through Whom does a person come?
Answer	**Yeshua**
Question	To Whom does a person come?
Answer	**To the Father**

Each question asked helped to break up the basic components of the passage, thus positioning the reader to understand more. This works with simple passages like John 14:6, and it works with more complicated passages, too. With larger portions of scripture, repeated readings may be necessary, and thus, reinforce the truth.

To study scripture, please remember these points:
- **Always begin with prayer.** Use the Bible Study to intensify and escalate your relationship with the Almighty.
- **Spend time praying about any passage.** Should you find you do not understand it, ask the Holy Spirit to guide you to unlock the truth. While commentaries can be helpful and sometimes clarify difficult passages, please do not make them your first place of investigation. Pray and ask God to show you, first. Then, investigate.
- **Look at passages set in their original language.** At times, certain passages require a little more clarity, so they must be considered within

---

[2] Most students find this a little hard to do, however, in the long run this habit reaps great rewards.

their original language and cultural setting. (e.g., Hebraic scriptures (First Covenant[3]) or Apostolic Scriptures (Second Covenant). To do that, find a good online bible program that gives you the root word. Using KJV makes looking up the root words easy, since Strong's Exhaustive Concordance co-relates nicely with the KJV.

- **Keep passages within their original setting**. When reading the text in the Chapters, if the passage is not familiar to you, go to your Bible and read the passage within its setting of chapter and book.
- **Be honest in answering any personal questions asked**. If studying in a group and asked to share, if your answer seems too personal or difficult to share, simply tell the teacher that you prefer to pass on this one.
- **Encourage yourself when needed**. Whenever you encounter Chapters requiring lots of time, or you feel overwhelmed, take some time to pray and think about the passages. Remember the old riddle asked to a young child: "How do you eat an elephant?". Remember the answer: one bite at a time! Thus, approach long Chapters by answering one question at a time until finished. To benefit from scripture at any time in your life, "read the text (scriptures) and do what it says". In that, you will find fulfilment in your God and your faith, confident how to live it out, victoriously.

"Be doers and not hearers only of the Word of God" [4]

- **Time constraints**:
    - *Accredited students*, consider doing the homework by meting it out in a daily allotment. You might consider an hour or two a day.
    - *Unaccredited students*, split your time in doing your study as best suits your schedule.

No matter how you decide to do your homework, remember, the idea is not to see how quickly you can get it done. Rather, use the workbook as a tool to get to know the Word and its author better.

---

[3] The book of Hebrews, when referring to the Hebraic written scriptures, refers to them as the First Covenant.
[4] Based on James 1:22

USE OF CERTAIN TERMS

As we study the Word of God, together, there are a few terms that we might use, whose meaning might change depending on circumstances. To ensure we are on the same page, please familiarize yourself with these terms:

- **YeHoVaH, YHVH**: In ancient Hebrew manuscripts, scribes wrote the Hebrew name of God as יְהֹוָה. Today's manuscripts use LORD. Cëgullah Publishing uses the word "YeHoVaH" or YHVH – meaning the yod, hey, vav, hey of the Hebrew letters. For more information on this subject, please see the Appendix of the textbook.
- **Yeshua**: According to the angel, our Saviour's name was Yehoshua. We shorten that name to Yeshua, just like we shorten names such as James to Jim. Thus, we honour Yeshua with His Hebrew name, as much as possible.
- **Messiah:** The Hebrew word for Messiah means anointed One, which, when speaking of the Messiah, refers to Yeshua. In Greek, the word "Christ" is used, which actually means "smeared with grease." We prefer to use the Hebrew word, Messiah, again as we see this as more honouring to Yeshua.
- **Church:** Whenever we use the word "Church", we do not speak of any building, but it is a reference in general to those who profess Christianity.
- **Ekklesia:** This word refers to the body of believers gathered from the world to serve God. It refers to all who call themselves believers.
- **Remnant**: A remnant differs from church and ekklesia in that it refers to those who, like the prophets in the time of Elijah, did not bow their knees to Baal. Today, these are true believers as God sees them.
- **Man:** Scripture refers often to "man", meaning humankind. Unless the passage itself refers to a particular male person, apply the passage to all humankind. For example, if **any man** is in Christ, he is a new creation. Interpret that to mean if **any person** is in Messiah, they are a new creation.
- **First Covenant**: When referring to the Covenant under Moses, scripture calls that covenant, "the first covenant" not Old Covenant. So do we.

Hopefully, understanding these few terms will keep us on the same page!

Before closing this note, please understand that your primary goal to study God's Word is to get to know the God of the Bible. This comes, slowly, as you read the Bible and prayerfully connect with Him. To put it another way, you intentionally take time to study His Word, reading it slowly with faith, knowing that the Holy Spirit helps you learn its meaning. To do so brings forth fruit which produces *life* in you for God's Word are Spirit and life! That life produces evidence that you have been with God! It is a valuable treasure deposited in your life, which otherwise does not come to you!

Beloved, do not be content just to listen to others teach, expound, or present His Word to you! Study it for yourself!

In light of your faith walk with God, dear reader, there is nothing more powerful, inspiring, or rewarding than connecting with God through His Living Word, *a category in which the written Word falls.*

Dear one, I realize we lead busy lives, some more busy than others. However, time management becomes paramount when connecting with God, and His Word must take an important priority. Prayerfully, ask God to help you, faithfully and consistently study His Word. Ask Him if you need to set some other thing aside in order to give the Word of God the priority in your life that He desires. Freeing your time to study the Word brings with it such a rewarding satisfaction as He blesses you for your determination to know His Word and learn of Him and His ways.

Please consider these helps as you move forward to read, study, grow and connect with the Living God!

Richest blessings.

Jeanne

Jeanne Metcalf – President and CEO
Cegullah Publishing & Apologetic Academy Inc.
www.cegullahpublishing.ca

COURSE 302
INDEX

CHAPTER	TITLE	PAGE
	SECTION 1: CITIZENSHIP	
	Heads Up!..	17
	Pre-Course Study Information…………………..	17
1	Kingdom Mysteries	23
2	Kingdom Entrance...	41
3	Kingdom Realities...	53
4	Kingdom Laws...	67
	SECTION 2: AMBASSADORSHIP	
5	Kingdom Inheritance...	89
6	Kingdom Ambassadors.......................................	103
7	Kingdom Government...	115

COURSE 303

	SECTION 3: STEWARDSHIP	
8	Kingdom Priorities..	131
9	Kingdom Blessings...	141
10	Kingdom Authority..	155
11	Kingdom Keys...	165
12	Kingdom Treasures...	181

APPENDIX

About Cegullah Publishing...	214
Contact...	214
Scripture Index..	211

Hebrew Word Study

Ambassador.................	198	Law............................	205
Bless.............................	199	Love...........................	206
Curse............................	200	Name..........................	207
Dominion.....................	201	Peculiar Treasure...........	208
Faith............................	202	Throne........................	209
Heart............................	203	Watchers.....................	210
Judgment.....................	204		

COURSE 302

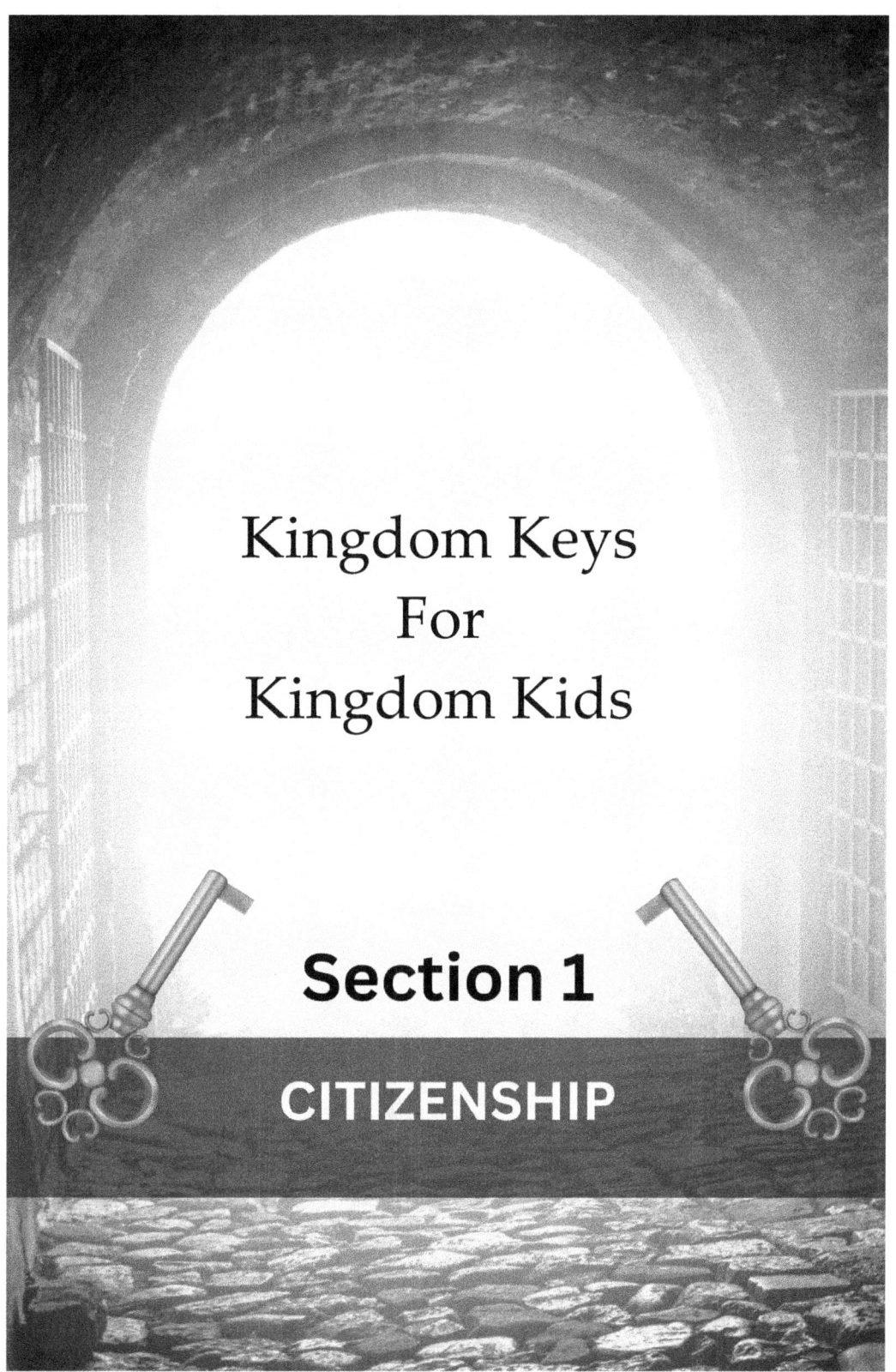

Kingdom Keys For Kingdom Kids

Section 1

CITIZENSHIP

Heads Up!

Attention All Students:

Most of our *unaccredited students* are free to take our study courses in any order they desire. However, our accredited students must follow the yearly plan. Therefore, the information on the following pages act like a review to accredited students, and depending on the unaccredited course order, may be review to those students as well.

Pre-Course Study
Information

A. ORIGINAL BIBLE TRANSCRIPTS

Since God gave the Bible to His People in a language, other than English, it is important for those English-speaking people studying the Bible to understand that God guaranteed Divine Inspiration in the original transcripts, not in English Bible translations. Ardent Bible students need to realize that fact and then look at the original transcripts of the Bible for clarity, but not everyone has the education to do that. Thus, over the years, scholars prepared materials for the average person to use as an aid to understand the meaning of the original words. One of the best sources is Strong's Exhaustive Concordance. Its author identified all the root words of the Hebraic Scriptures and Apostolic Scriptures, assigned a number to each word, and then gave a broad explanation of that word in English to help students understand the original message the word conveyed.

One further aid to understanding the original transcripts comes from a recent discovery by scholars who uncovered the original pictograph language used in ancient times. This discovery further expands the original concept of the Hebrew Words. While the basic meaning of many of those Hebrew words may not be even identical to Modern Hebrew, it does open our understanding to grasp some concepts of its ancient meaning and gives a broader view of the deeper things in the Word of God.

Since this book refers to the Ancient Pictograph Language, we include here a short explanation on that language for the reader to review. It is in no way a complete study but is merely an overview to help the student grasp the concept of the ancient picture language and explains why it is used in this book.

B. THE ANCIENT PICTURE LANGUAGE[5]

Whenever you translate something from one language to another, there is always a risk of compromising the depth of the original language, especially if that language is not as expressive as the original, and does not hold words, which precisely articulate the meaning. Such is the case when translating from Hebrew to English. For example, to translate a Hebrew 'tallit', which is an important part of the traditional Jewish garment, worn by men, we have no such English word to express it. The word tallit means, "little tent", but the translators simply interpreted it as tent. In our language, however, when we think of a tent, we know there are large tents and pup tents. However, 'tallit', if properly interpreted, is, in reality, a woven shawl traditionally made on a white background, in which people wrap themselves when they are in prayer alone with God. Today we call that a "prayer shawl". Translating the word, 'tallit' as 'tent', hardly means the same thing.

This is but one instance where early interpretations of scripture erred, and because of that one little mistake, many believers think that Acts 18:3, which described the

---

[5] Normally, we include some information about the Hebrew Picture Language, however, this course introduction covers this aspect. Chapter 1 of the textbook explains it well, therefore, feel free to skip past this part.

Introduction

Apostle Paul as abiding with 'tentmakers', means that Paul made tents, meaning outdoor shelters, when in fact, as a trained Pharisee, Paul made prayer shawls. This is but one instance but there are many other places in the Word, where translators overlooked cultural expressions and the like, and thus, gave the reader a different meaning than the original transcripts.

We must always ensure, when looking at Hebrew words with our English mind, that we consider these things and remember that *Hebraic thinking differs greatly from our Western world.* Differences in thinking, between Hebraic and Western thought, would take a lot of time to explain, so for now, keep in mind, that the Hebraic language is 'relational' while the Western World is not. The Hebrew picture language explains that point well.

C. AN AGRICULTURAL, RELATIONSHIP-BASED LANGUAGE[6]

The early Hebrew language, like other languages, began as an *agriculturally based language* explaining ideas of their civilization with 'pictures' relative to their environment. The alphabet, in this early language, was comprised of letters, whose design indicated certain parts of the body to describe certain words. Other letters used well-known animals, such as the ox and others, to describe common things during their civilization's existence. For example, the letter "aleph", the first letter, pictured an ox's head, and the second letter "bet" represented a tent where the family lived. To explain this in further detail, we will look at the word, "father", which uses both the "aleph" and the "bet".

THE HEBREW WORD FOR FATHER

Hebrew words usually have a base of three characters. The first two characters are known as Parent Root, the characters following are known as

---

[6] To learn more about the pictograph language, see Dr. Seekins book, entitled, Hebrew Word Pictures, ISBN 13: 978-0-967972-61-9.

the Child Root. [7] The word for father is "Ab". In English as you can see, there are two letters, A and b. In the Hebrew, in this case, there are also two letters, but they are not A and b, but ALEPH and BET. In order to read the Hebrew, there is something you must remember and that is the direction in which to read Hebrew.

In English, we read this way ⟶ from Left to Right,
In Hebrew, we read this way ⟵ from Right to Left.

For us, this seems rather awkward, but nevertheless, keep that in mind as you read the letters below.

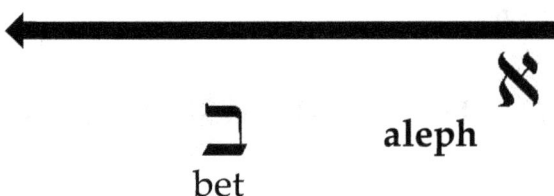

In the picture language, an Ox's head represents the Aleph, and the Bet is pictured as a dwelling place, or a tent. The **ox** is a strong animal, used to pull carts and carry heavy burdens and the like. Within a tent, the family lived. Putting this together, you have a picture of a strong person, capable of carrying burdens, caring for the family. Hence, the Hebrew picture language describes the father as this: *The strong person over the family, or to put it another way, a father is the strong one of the house*[8].

Keep in mind that the pictograph language, in Hebrew, is relational, rather than abstract as in the English language. A study of it produces amazing thoughts from which we can learn much.

PROPER USE OF THE PICTURE LANGUAGE

---

[7] When understanding "Parent and Child Root" it is only in the most simplistic format that it is easy to interpret. Past four or five characters, it is more difficult to grasp.
[8] Dr. Seekins interprets this slightly differently. To know more, consider purchasing his book, Hebrew Word Pictures. ISBN 13: 978-0-967972-61-9.

Introduction

Throughout this study, we will look at many Hebrew words in order to obtain a deeper meaning of the Word. As you learn some of those deeper meanings, please realize that you cannot automatically substitute that broader meaning of that word whenever you come across the same English word in the version of scripture that you read. When translating the Bible, scholars may have used the same English word for two or three different Hebrew words. For example, in the Hebrew Scriptures, we find two major words that mean peace. Once word is שלום, pronounced Shalom. This word is familiar to many of us. Expanding it to the ancient picture language, it means "to break every authority causing chaos". With the absence of chaos, the result is peace. The other Hebrew word is חרש, pronounced khaw-rash. This word, many do not know. Its picture in the ancient pictograph language suggests blocking words that come from the head, or in other words, it means speechless, to remain silent. Here again is a picture of peace, but not the same in context as the first word in Hebrew, nor of our idea of peace in English.

When looking at Hebrew words from the ancient, pictograph language, ensure that you observe some basic rules. Unless you are a Hebrew scholar, with a good understanding of sentence structure, only use the expanded meaning to apply to the immediate subject at hand. Also, ensure its meaning fits well within the context of other scriptures giving reference to the same topic.

If you follow these simple rules, you should do fine!

IMPORTANT INFORMATION ABOUT A STRONG'S CONCORDANCE.	
When using a concordance to look up Hebrew &Greek words online or by hand in a book, please remember:	
The Hebraic Scriptures are the First Covenant.	Originally, this covenant was written in Hebrew or Hebrew/Chaldean and while it is similar to modern day Hebrew, it differs somewhat from the language spoken today in Israel.
The Apostolic Scriptures are the New Covenant.	Most of today's Christian world believes these Apostolic scriptures written in Koine Greek. Other scholars today, however, believe the original, early manuscripts were written in Hebrew. *Nevertheless,* until these come forward, we use the Greek Koine Greek language in which to look back at the Apostolic Scriptures.
When looking up these words in a Concordance, the following system is often used:	G plus the # = Greek Words e.g., G2875 H plus the # = Hebrew Words e.g. H2875. Some computers use a "0" rather than the H

KINGDOM MYSTERIES 1

This Chapter includes scriptures used in the Textbook Introduction as well as textbook Chapter 1.

INSTRUCTIONS: In every chapter of this workbook, please begin with prayer and then, use the scripture in the workbook as a lesson of learning between you and your God! If you are not familiar with a certain passage, then go to your Bible and read some surrounding text.

Read the questions and answer them to the best of your ability. Whenever a question asks for *your opinion*, feel free to right down your honest viewpoint on the subject, and be sure to add in your scriptural reference to support your viewpoint.

PLEASE NOTE:
If question throughout the workbook asks for a yes or no and gives little space, just answer the question. However, if space is given for more than a yes or no answer, please explain the reason for your answer, using scripture to support your viewpoint.

1 Corinthians 3:19-4:1
"**19** For the wisdom of this world is foolishness with God. For it is written, He taketh the wise in their own craftiness. **20** And again, The Lord knoweth the thoughts of the wise, that they are vain. **21** ¶ Therefore let no man glory in men. For all things are yours; **22** Whether Paul, or Apollos, or Cephas, or the world, or life, or death, or things present, or things to come; all are yours; **23** And ye are Christ's; and Christ *is* God's. **4:1** ¶ Let a man so account of us, as of the ministers of Christ, and stewards of the mysteries of God."

1.	Question	What is the wisdom of this world to God? (vs 19
	Answer	
2.	Question	What was written? (Job 5:13. a quote from the First Covenant) (vs 19)
	Answer	
3.	Question	What does YHVH know? (vs 20) [2 things]
	Answer	
4.	Question	Therefore, what shall no man do and why? (vs 21)
	Answer	
5.	Question	Verse 22 explains "what are ours". List those things.
	Answer	
6.	Question	Recap verse 23 to 4:1.
	Answer	

Ephesians 1:15-23
"**15** Wherefore I also, after I heard of your faith in the Lord Jesus, and love unto all the saints, **16** Cease not to give thanks for you, making mention of you in my prayers; **17** That the God of our Lord Jesus Christ, the Father of glory, may give unto you the spirit of wisdom and revelation in the

knowledge of him: **18** The eyes of your understanding being enlightened; that ye may know what is the hope of his calling, and what the riches of the glory of his inheritance in the saints, **19** And what *is* the exceeding greatness of his power to us-ward who believe, according to the working of his mighty power, **20** Which he wrought in Christ, when he raised him from the dead, and set *him* at his own right hand in the heavenly *places*, **21** Far above all principality, and power, and might, and dominion, and every name that is named, not only in this world, but also in that which is to come: **22** And hath put all *things* under his feet, and gave him *to be* the head over all *things* to the church, **23** Which is his body, the fulness of him that filleth all in all."

7.	QUESTION:	What did the Apostle Paul, the author of Ephesians, do after he heard of the faith of the saints at Ephesus? (vs 16)
	ANSWER:	
8.	COMMENT:	You will study the teaching in this prayer in Chapter 5.
	QUESTION:	Summarize Paul's petition. (vs 17-22)
	ANSWER:	

		Continue your answer here.

Ephesians 2:15		
"a) Having abolished in his flesh the enmity, *even* the law of commandments *contained* in ordinances; b) for to make in himself of twain one new man, c) *so* making peace;"		
9.	QUESTION:	What did God abolish in His flesh? (vs 15 a) (1 word)
	ANSWER:	
10.	QUESTION:	Why did He do that? (vs 15 b)
	ANSWER:	
11.	QUESTION:	What resulted from God's action? (15 c) (1 word)
	ANSWER:	
12.	QUESTION:	Looking at the 1 word answer from verse 15 a), **compare it** with the 1 word answer in verse 15 c. (e.g are they similar or different and if so, how?)
	ANSWER:	

13.	QUESTION:	What, therefore, is the benefit of making "one new man"? (Hint: think about Adam who formerly existed, and all in him, (which includes both Jew and Gentile) and their ultimate end, compared to the Last Adam, and all in Him and their ultimate end.)[9]
	ANSWER:	

Mark 4:11-12

"**11** And he said unto them, Unto you it is given to know the mystery of the kingdom of God: but unto them that are without, all *these* things are done in parables: **12** That seeing they may see, and not perceive; and hearing they may hear, and not understand; lest at any time they should be converted, and *their* sins should be forgiven them."

14.	QUESTION:	What is given to believers? (vs 11)
	ANSWER:	

---

[9] If you want to check out your answer, read the footnote to this scripture in the textbook, but only after you tried to answer it!

15.	QUESTION:	What is the unbelieving given? (vs 11)
	ANSWER:	
16.	QUESTION:	Why are they given this? (vs 12)
	ANSWER:	

Matthew 11:12
"And from the days of John the Baptist until now the kingdom of heaven suffereth violence, and the violent take it by force."

17.	QUESTION:	What did the kingdom of heaven suffer?
	ANSWER:	
18.	QUESTION:	What took it by force?
	ANSWER:	

Luke 8:9-10
9 And his disciples asked him, saying, What might this parable be? **10** And he said, Unto you it is given to know the mysteries of the kingdom of God: but to others in parables; that seeing they might not see, and hearing they might not understand.

19.	Question	Yeshua spoke the parable of the sower to His listening audience. Later, when He was alone with His disciples, they asked Him a question. Verse 9 above records that question. What question did they ask Yeshua?

	Answer	
20.	Question	To whom does the "unto you" refer? (vs 10)
	Answer	
21.	Question	What was it that is given to them to know? (vs 10)
	Answer	
22.	Question	Do you think Yeshua's statement applied only to those in His immediate listening audience? Explain your reasoning.
	Answer	
23.	Question	In your own words, describe what you consider the mysteries of the Kingdom of God.
	Answer	

Romans 8:5-9
"**5** For they that are after the flesh do mind the things of the flesh; but they that are after the Spirit the things of the Spirit. **6** For to be carnally minded *is* death; but to be spiritually minded *is* life and peace. **7** Because the carnal mind *is* enmity against God: for it is not subject to the law of God, neither indeed can be. **8** So then they that are in the flesh cannot please God. **9** But ye are not in the flesh, but in the Spirit, if so be that the Spirit of God dwell in you. Now if any man have not the Spirit of Christ, he is none of his."

24.	Question	What do these "after the flesh" obey? (vs 5)
	Answer	
25.	Question	What do those "after the Spirit" obey? (vs 5)
	Answer	
26.	Question	What happens to those who are carnally[10] minded? (vs 6)
	Answer	
27.	Question	What happens to those who are spiritually[11] minded? (vs 6)
	Answer	
28.	Question	Why are these things so? (vs 7 explains)
	Answer	
29.	Question	How does God look upon those who live only for the flesh? (vs 8)
	Answer	
30.	Question	If the Spirit is in a believer, what does verse 9 conclude?
	Answer	

---

[10] To be carnally minded is to think after the things of the flesh.
[11] These are things of the Holy Spirit and of the Kingdom of God.

Chapter 1 — Kingdom Mysteries

Hebrews 11:6

6 But without faith *it is* impossible to please *him*: for he that cometh to God must believe that he is, and *that* he is a rewarder of them that diligently seek him."

31.	Question	What pleases God, according to Hebrews 11:6?
	Answer	
32.	Question	How does one come to God?
	Answer	
33.	Question	What happens when one seeks God diligently?
	Answer	

Jeremiah 29:13

13 And ye shall seek me, and find *me*, when ye shall search for me with all your heart.

34.	Question	Jeremiah, the Prophet, spoke these words to Judah, on behalf of the Lord. When one seeks God, what condition must be met to ensure they will find Him?
	Answer	

1 Corinthians 2:14

14 But the natural man receiveth not the things of the Spirit of God: for they are foolishness unto him: neither can he know *them*, because they are spiritually discerned."

35.	Question	Does the natural man receive things of the Spirit of God? (vs 14)

	Answer	
36.	Question	How do they perceive the things of the Spirit of God? (vs 14)
	Answer	
37.	Question	How does one perceive the spirituals things of God? (vs 14)
	Answer	

Romans 1:20		
20 a) For the invisible things of him from the creation of the world are clearly seen, b) being understood by the things that are made, c) *even* his eternal power and Godhead; so that they are without excuse:		
38.	Question	What does verse 20 a) say about invisible things?
	Answer	
39.	Question	Still referring to invisible things, how do we understand these them? (vs 20 b)
	Answer	
40.	Question	Verse 20 c) states two things that are invisible to man. What are those two things?
	Answer	

41..	Question	What does verse 20 c) conclude?
	Answer	
42.	Question	Try to put the meaning of this verse into your own words.
	Answer	

Exodus 18:16		
16 When they have a matter, they come unto me; and I judge between one and another, and I do make them know the statutes of God, and his laws.		
43.	COMMENT	Moses spoke to Jethro, his father-in-law, explaining what it was that he did daily.
	Question	What two things does Moses state here about his daily doings? (vs 16
	Answer	

Ezra 7:25		
25 And thou, Ezra, after the wisdom of thy God, that is in thine hand, set magistrates and judges, which may judge all the people that are beyond the river, all such as know the laws of thy God; and teach ye them that know them not.		
44.	COMMENT	Ezra received a commission from the King of Persia to return to Jerusalem.

	Question	List the things that the King appointed for Ezra to do.
	Answer	

Psalm 105:40-45		
40 The people asked, and he brought quails, and satisfied them with the bread of heaven. 41 He opened the rock, and the waters gushed out; they ran in the dry places like a river. 42 For he remembered his holy promise, and Abraham his servant. 43 And he brought forth his people with joy, and his chosen with gladness: 44 And gave them the lands of the heathen: and they inherited the labour of the people; 45 That they might observe his statutes and keep his laws. Praise ye YeHoVaH.		
45.	Question	What does it say regarding God's Laws? (vs 45)
	Answer	

Psalm 139:7-13		
7 ¶ Whither shall I go from your spirit? or whither shall I flee from your presence? 8 If I ascend up into heaven, thou art there: if I make my bed in hell, behold, thou art there. 9 If I take the wings of the morning, and dwell in the uttermost parts of the sea; 10 Even there shall your hand lead me, and your right hand shall hold me. 11 If I say, Surely the darkness shall cover me; even the night shall be light about me. 12 Yea, the darkness hides not from you; but the night shines as the day: the darkness and the light are both alike to you. 13 For thou hast possessed my reins: thou hast covered me in my mother's womb.		
46.	Question	After reading the scripture above, name 4 (four) places where one cannot escape from God's Presence.

	Answer	

Matthew 3:1-2		
1 ¶ In those days came John the Baptist, preaching in the wilderness of Judaea, **2** And saying, Repent ye: for the kingdom of heaven is at hand.		
47.	Question	What message did John the Baptist preach?
	Answer	

Luke 17:20-21		
20 ¶ And when he was demanded of the Pharisees, when the Kingdom of God should come, he answered them and said, The Kingdom of God cometh not with observation: 21 Neither shall they say, Lo here! or, lo there! for, behold, the Kingdom of God is within you.		
48.	Question	What did the Pharisees wish to know? (vs 20)
	Answer	

Kingdom Keys for Kingdom Kids   Walking in Kingdom Power

49.	Question	What answer did Yeshua give them? (vs 20-21)
	Answer	
50..	Question	Explain that answer in your own words.
	Answer	

That finishes the Bible verses for this section. Before closing, turn to the Appendix. Look up the word "Law". Write a quick recap of that word in the space below. If you need more space, use loose leaf paper.

51.	Law
52.	Do you think it is important to know the Laws of the country in which you live? Write out your answer in the provided space. (If you are stuck on how to explain this, think about what happens if a country has no laws!)

Chapter 1 — Kingdom Mysteries

	(continue your answer here)
53.	God's Kingdom, like any other kingdom, has laws. In the space below, write out a summary of the laws you presently know that operate in the Kingdom of God. .

PRECIOUS MOMENTS RECAP

54.	QUESTION:	Review this workbook chapter. Pick out the scriptures that spoke to you the most. Write at least one of those scriptures in the space below.
	ANSWER:	
55.	QUESTION:	What specific truth from the scriptures you studied in this workbook chapter speaks to you. Write that truth in the space below.
	ANSWER:	

Chapter 1 | Kingdom Mysteries

		(continue your answer here)
56.	QUESTION:	Think of how you can apply this scripture to your life. Enter those thoughts in the space below.
	ANSWER:	

		(continue your answer here)

Chapter 2　　　　　　　　　　　　　　　　　　　Kingdom Entrance

KINGDOM ENTRANCE　　2

REMEMBER:
- Begin with **Prayer**.
- Use the scripture in the workbook as a lesson of learning between you and your God!
- If you are not familiar with a certain passage, then go to your Bible and read some surrounding text.

John 3:1-7
1 ¶ There was a man of the Pharisees, named Nicodemus, a ruler of the Jews: **2** The same came to Jesus by night, and said unto him, Rabbi, we know that thou art a teacher come from God: for no man can do these miracles that thou doest, except God be with him. **3** Jesus answered and said unto him, Verily, verily, I say unto thee, Except a man be born again, *he cannot see the kingdom of God*. **4** Nicodemus saith unto him, How can a man be born when he is old? can he enter the second time into his mother's womb, and be born? **5** Jesus answered, Verily, verily, I say unto thee, Except a man be born of water and *of* the Spirit, *he cannot enter into the kingdom of God*. **6** That which is born of the flesh is flesh; and that which is born of the Spirit is spirit. **7** Marvel not that I said unto thee, *Ye must be born again*."

1.	Question	Who came to speak to Yeshua, and what position did that man hold? (vs 1)
	Answer	

Kingdom Keys for Kingdom Kids   Walking in Kingdom Power

2.	Question	What comment did the man make as recorded by verse 2?
	Answer	
3.	Question	What did Yeshua say to the man regarding the Kingdom of God? (vs 3)
	Answer	
4. .	Question	The man did not understand the answer, so he asked another question. Yeshua responded with another statement. What was that statement? (vs 5 only)
	Answer	
5.	Question	What comment did Yeshua make as recorded in verse 6?
	Answer	
6.	Question	Yeshua said that the man should not marvel about something. What was that something?
	Answer	
7.	Question	There are three major comments of extreme importance within this passage of scripture. Read it again. List the three major comments in the space below.

Chapter 2 — Kingdom Entrance

	Answer	i	
		ii	
		iii	

Mark 1:14-15		
14 Now after that John was put in prison, Jesus came into Galilee, preaching the gospel of the Kingdom of God, 15 And saying, The time is fulfilled, and the Kingdom of God is at hand: repent you, and believe the gospel.		
8.	Question	After John was in prison, what does verse 14 tell us about Yeshua? (vs 14 only)
	Answer	
9.	Question	What message did Yeshua speak? (vs 15)
	Answer	
10.	Question	What did Yeshua say about the Kingdom of God?
	Answer	

11.	Question	What do you think is important about Yeshua's statement regarding the Kingdom of God?
	Answer	

Matthew 7:21
21 Not everyone that says unto me, Lord, Lord, shall enter into the kingdom of heaven; but he that does the will of my Father which is in heaven.

12.	Question	Who shall enter the Kingdom of Heaven?
	Answer	

13.	**COMMENT**	You read this scripture earlier: John 3: **5** Jesus answered, Verily, verily, I say unto thee, Except a man be born of water and *of the Spirit, he cannot enter into the kingdom of God.* **6** That which is born of the flesh is flesh; and that which is born of the Spirit is spirit. **7** Marvel not that I said unto thee, *Ye must be born again.* Think about it, and then re-read Matthew 7:21 (Written before question # 12)
	Question	Is there any relationship between Matthew 7:21 and John 3:5-7? (*Hint: identify the main thoughts of both scriptures, then answer*)
	Answer	

		Continue your answer here

Mark 12:29-31		
29 And Jesus answered him, The first of all the commandments is, Hear, O Israel; YeHoVaH our God is one Lord: 30 And you shall love YeHoVaH your God with all your heart, and with all your soul, and with all your mind, and with all your strength: this is the first commandment. 31 And the second is like, namely this, you shall love your neighbour as yourself. There is none other commandment greater than these.		
14.	Question	What is the first commandment? (vs 30)
	Answer	
15.	Question	What is the second commandment? (vs 31)

John 20:30-31		
30 And many other signs truly did Jesus in the presence of his disciples, which are not written in this book: 31 But these are written, that you might believe that Jesus is the Christ, the Son of God; and that believing you might have life through his name.		
16.	Question	Why did John write about the "signs" that Yeshua did in the presence of His disciples?

	Answer	
17.	Question	What happens when one believes in Yeshua as the Messiah (the Christ)?
	Answer	

Romans 10:8-13
8 But what says it *(the scriptures)*? The word is near you, even in your mouth, and in your heart: that is, the word of faith, which we preach; 9 That if you shall confess with your mouth the Lord Jesus and shall believe in the Lord Jesus and hath raised him from the dead, you shall be saved. 10 For with the heart man believes unto righteousness; and with the mouth confession is made unto salvation. 11 For the scripture says, Whosoever believes on him shall not be ashamed. 12 ¶ For there is no difference between the Jew and the Greek: for the same Lord over all is rich unto all that call upon him. 13 For whosoever shall call upon the name of the Lord shall be saved.

18.	Question	Where is the Word of God? (vs 8)
	Answer	
19.	Question	What did they preach? (vs 8 only)

Chapter 2 — Kingdom Entrance

20.	Question	What was the "faith message"? (vs 9)
	Answer	

21.	Question	How does man believe? (vs 10)

22.	Question	How is salvation realized? (vs 10)
	Answer	

23.	Question	What does verse 11 say that the scripture says?
	Answer	

24.	Question	What does verse 12 say regarding Jew and Greek[12]?
	Answer	

25.	Question	What does is say about the Lord? (vs 12)
	Answer	

---

[12] In the Jewish mind, there were two types of people. They were either Jew or Greek, Jew or Gentile, Bond or Free, Saved or Unsaved.

26.	Question	What does it say about crying out to the Lord? (vs 13)
	Answer	

Matthew 5:3		
3 Blessed [are] the poor in spirit: for theirs is the kingdom of heaven."		
27.	Question	What does it say regarding the Kingdom of heaven[13]? (vs 3)
	Answer	

Turn to the APPENDIX. Locate the following Hebrew Words. Read about the *possible Hebrew depths* of those words, then recap their content in the space below.

28.	Ambassador	

---

[13] Kingdom of God and Kingdom of Heaven are often synonymous terms.

Chapter 2　　　　　　　　　　　　　　　　　　　　Kingdom Entrance

29.	Bless	
30.	Curse	

PRECIOUS MOMENTS RECAP

31.	QUESTION:	Review this workbook chapter. Pick out the scriptures that spoke to you the most. Write at least one of those scriptures in the space below.
	ANSWER:	

		(continue your answer here)
32.	QUESTION:	What specific truth from the scriptures you studied in this workbook chapter speaks to you. Write that truth in the space below.
	ANSWER:	

Chapter 2											Kingdom Entrance

		(continue your answer here)
33.	QUESTION:	Think of how you can apply this scripture to your life. Enter those thoughts in the space below.
	ANSWER:	

KINGDOM REALITIES 3

REMEMBER:
- Begin with Prayer.
- Use the scripture in the workbook as a lesson of learning between you and your God!
- If you are not familiar with a certain passage, then go to your Bible and read some surrounding text.

James 1:17-18		
17 Every good gift and every perfect gift is from above, and cometh down from the Father of Lights, with whom is no variableness[14], neither shadow of turning. 18 Of his own will begat he us with the word of truth, that we should be a kind of firstfruits of his creatures.		
1.	Question	From where does every good and perfect gift originate? (vs 17)
	Answer	
2.	Question	Vs 17 speaks some things about the "Father of Lights". What does it say about Him?
3.	Question	Explain the importance of knowing these things about the Father of Lights.
	Answer	

---

[14] One who is variable, is one who constantly changes. This is not the character of YeHoVaH!

4.	Question	"Begat" refers to fathering a child. How did the Father of life (obtain) beget us? (vs 18)
	Answer	
5.	Question	Why did He do that? (vs 18)
	Answer	

2 Corinthians 5:17		
17 Therefore if any man be in Christ, he is a new creature[15]: old things are passed away; behold, all things are become new.		
6.	Question	What is a person in Messiah (Christ)? (vs 17)
	Answer	
7.	Question	Why do you think Paul, the writer of this letter to the Corinthians, thought it important to mention that those in Messiah were a new creation, something that never before existed?
	Answer	
8.	Question	What happened to old things? (vs 17)
	Answer	
9.	Question	What happens to all things? (vs 17)
	Answer	

---

[15] This means a new creation. It is something that never before existed.

Chapter 3 Kingdom Realities

2 Peter 1:4		
4 a) Whereby are given unto us exceeding great and precious promises: b) that by these you might be *partakers of the divine nature*, c) having escaped the corruption that is in the world through lust.		
10.	Question	What is given to believers, according to verse 4 a)?
	Answer	
11.	Question	Why is this given to believers? (vs 4 b)
12.	Question	What have believers escaped? (vs 4 c)
	Answer	

Daniel 2:20-22		
20 Daniel answered and said, Blessed be the name of God for ever and ever: for wisdom and might are his: 21 And he changeth the times and the seasons: he removeth kings, and setteth up kings: he giveth wisdom unto the wise, and knowledge to them that know understanding: 22 He revealeth the deep and secret things: he knoweth what [is] in the darkness, and the light dwelleth with him.		
13.	Question	According to verse 20, what belongs to God?
	Answer	
14.	Question	What does God **change** according to verse 21?
	Answer	

Kingdom Keys for Kingdom Kids   Walking in Kingdom Power

15.	Question	What does God remove? (vs 21)
	Answer	
16.	Question	Whom does God set up (put in power)? (vs 21)
	Answer	
17.	Question	What does God give to the wise and those that know understanding? (vs 21)
	Answer	
18.	Question	What does God reveal? (vs 22)
	Answer	
19.	Question	What specifics of God's knowledge does verse 22 relate?
	Answer	
20.	Question	Where does the Light dwell? (vs 22)
	Answer	

Deuteronomy 29:29		
29 a) The secret things belong unto YeHoVaH our God: b) but those things which are revealed belong unto us and to our children for ever, c) that we may do all the words of this law.		
21.	Question	What does verse 29 a) declares about the Lord?
	Answer	

Chapter 3   Kingdom Realities

22.	Question	What does verse 29 b) say about "us and our children"?
23.	Question	Why does God reveal these things? (vs 29 c)
	Answer	

THE PARABLE OF THE SOWER
Mark 4:3-9
3 Hearken[16]; Behold[17] there went out a sower to sow[18]: 4 And it came to pass, as he sowed, some fell by the wayside, and the fowls of the air came and devoured it up. 5 And some fell on stony ground, where it had not much earth; and immediately it sprang up, because it had no depth of earth: 6 But when the sun was up, it was scorched; and because it had no root, it withered away. 7 And some fell among thorns, and the thorns grew up, and choked it, and it yielded no fruit. 8 And other fell on good ground, and did yield fruit that sprang up and increased; and brought forth, some thirty, and some sixty, and some an hundred. 9 And he said unto them, He that hath ears to hear, let him hear.

24.	Question	This parable is about a farmer who sowed seed. What happened to the seed that fell along the wayside? (vs 4)
	Answer	

---

[16] Listen
[17] Look
[18] Remember, he takes the seed in his hand and scatters it as he goes along.

Kingdom Keys for Kingdom Kids — Walking in Kingdom Power

25.	Question	What happened to what fell upon stony ground? (vs 5-6)
	Answer	

26.	Question	What happened to those that fell among thorns? (vs 7)
	Answer	

27.	Question	What happened to those that fell among good ground? (vs 8)
	Answer	

28.	Question	How did Yeshua conclude this parable? (vs 9)
	Answer	

Mark 4:13

13 And he said unto them, Know ye not this parable? and how then will ye know all parables?

29.	Question	What question did Yeshua ask them?
	Answer	

30.	Question	Is this parable foundational to understand other parables? Explain your answer.
	Answer	

Chapter 3	Kingdom Realities

Mark 4:14-20
14 The sower soweth the word.

i.		15 And these are they by the way side, where the word is sown; but when they have heard, ha satan[19] cometh immediately, and taketh away the word that was sown in their hearts.
ii.		16 And these are they likewise which are sown on stony ground; who, when they have heard the word, immediately receive it with gladness; 17 And have no root in themselves, and so endure but for a time: afterward, when affliction or persecution ariseth for the word's sake, immediately they are offended.
iii.		18 And these are they which are sown among thorns; such as hear the word, 19 And the cares of this world, and the deceitfulness of riches, and the lusts of other things entering in, choke the word, and it becometh unfruitful.
iv.		20 And these are they which are sown on good ground; such as hear the word, and receive it, and bring forth fruit, some thirtyfold, some sixty, and some an hundred.

31.	Question	What does the sower do? (vs 14)
	Answer	
32.	Question	Who is the sower? (Give your best answer here, as later, we clarify it.)
	Answer	

---

[19] Means the adversary.

	Comment:	**IMPORTANT:** In your workbook, we divided the parable into 4 parts, labelling them i, ii, etc. Use those parts as a reference point in which to answer the following questions.
33.	Question	Explain those in category i).
	Answer	
34.	Question	Explain those in category ii).
	Answer	
35.	Question	Explain those in category iii).
36.	Question	Explain those in category iv).
	Answer	
37.	Question	How do you think one becomes part of the last category?

	Answer	

COMMENT: Remember, the Sower sows the Word. Keep that in mind as you read the next scripture and then answer the questions following it.

John 1:14		
14 And the Word was made flesh, and dwelt among us, (and we beheld his glory, the glory as of the only begotten of the Father,) full of grace and truth.		
38.	Question	Yeshua is the only begotten of the Father. Here it says He became flesh. What *else* does it say about Yeshua? (vs 14)
	Answer	
39.	Comment	**Yeshua is the Word of God. Therefore, in the parable of the sower, the sower are all those who sow Yeshua. (e.g. evangelists, preachers and teachers of the Word, etc.)**

39 cont'd	Question	Referring to the parable, summarize how people can hear and receive Yeshua.
	Answer	
40.	Question	Referring again to the parable, which way is the most fruitful?
	Answer	

Luke 8:21		
21 And he answered and said unto them, My mother and my brethren are these which hear the Word of God, and do it.		
41.	Question	Who are those Yeshua calls His family? (vs 21)
	Answer	

James 1:22		
22 But be you doers of the word, and not hearers only, deceiving your own selves		
42.	Question	What are believers to do? (vs 22)
	Answer	
43.	Question	If people hear the word and don't do it, what are they? (vs 22)
	Answer	

Chapter 3   Kingdom Realities

John 12:24-25		
4 Verily, verily, I say unto you, Except a corn of wheat fall into the ground and die, it abides alone: but if it die, it brings forth much fruit. 25 He that loves his life shall lose it; and he that hates his life in this world shall keep it unto life eternal.		
44.	Question	What happens to the corn of wheat that does not get put into the ground? (vs 24)
	Answer	
45.	Question	What happens when it is put into the ground? (vs 24)
	Answer	
46.	Question	What happens to the one that loves his life? (vs 25)
	Answer	
47.	Question	What happens to the one that loses his life in this world? (vs 25)
	Answer	

A look at a few Hebrew root words:

As before, turn to the Appendix. Look up the Hebrew word in its pictograph form. Recap its possible expanded meaning in the space provided.

48.	Faith

	Continue your answer here
49.	Heart
50.	Love

Chapter 4   Kingdom Laws

PRECIOUS MOMENTS RECAP

54.	QUESTION:	Review this workbook chapter. Pick out the scriptures that spoke to you the most. Write at least one of those scriptures in the space below.
	ANSWER:	
55.	QUESTION:	What specific truth from the scriptures you studied in this workbook chapter speaks to you. Write that truth in the space below.
	ANSWER:	

		(continue your answer here)
56.	QUESTION:	Think of how you can apply this scripture to your life. Enter those thoughts in the space below.
	ANSWER:	

KINGDOM LAWS 4

REMEMBER:
- Begin with Prayer.
- Use the scripture in the workbook as a lesson of learning between you and your God!
- If you are not familiar with a certain passage, then go to your Bible and read some surrounding text.

Colossians 1:12-13		
Colossians 1:		
12 Giving thanks unto the Father, which has made us **meet**[20] to be partakers of the inheritance of the saints in light[21]: 13 Who has delivered us from *the power of darkness, and hath translated us into the kingdom of his dear Son:*		
1.	Question	For what did God prepare us? (vs 12)
	Answer	
2.	Question	From what has He delivered us? (vs 13)

---

[20] "Meet" is an old-fashioned word, that today, we use infrequently, if at all. It means "sufficient". Looking further into the Greek Word from which this text originated, we note that the word "meet" carries with it the idea of fully equipped, with adequate power and ability to perform whatever duties are necessary, in any position where a person must function.

[21] Believers are called "saints" because they are set apart for God's purposes. In Colossians 1:12 believers are called saints in the Light, meaning, believers in the Kingdom of Light, or the Kingdom of God.

	Answer	
3.	Question	Where has He placed us?) vs 13)
	Answer	

Matthew 7:21
21 Not every one that says to me, Lord, Lord, shall enter into the kingdom of heaven; but he that does the will of my Father which is in heaven.

4.	Question	Who enters into the Kingdom of Heaven?
	Answer	

Matthew 21:28-32
28 ¶ But what think you? A certain man had two sons; and he came to the first, and said, Son, go work to day in my vineyard. 29 He answered and said, I will not: but afterward he repented, and went. 30 And he came to the second, and said likewise. And he answered and said, I go, sir: and went not. 31 Whether of the two did the will of his father? They say unto him, The first. Jesus said unto them, Verily I say unto you, That the publicans and the harlots go into the kingdom of God before you. 32 For John came unto you in the way of righteousness, and you believed him not: but the publicans and the harlots believed him: and you, when you had seen it, repented not afterward, that you might believe him.

5.	Question	Which son obeyed his father? Explain why. (vs 28-31)
	Answer	

Chapter 4   Kingdom Laws

6.	Question	Yeshua responded with a comment. Who did He say came into the Kingdom of God before the Jews? I(vs 31)
	Answer	
7.	Question	What did Yeshua say about John the Baptist? (vs 32)
	Answer	
8.	Question	Who did and who did not believe John? (vs 32)
	Answer	
9.	Question	What would happen if they repented?
	Answer	

Matthew 21:23
23 ¶ And when he was come into the temple, the chief priests and the elders of the people came unto him as he was teaching, and said, By what authority doest you these things? and who gave you this authority?

10.	Question	What questions did the chief priest and elders ask Yeshua? (vs 23)
	Answer	

John 3:16		
16 a) For God so loved the world, b) that he gave his only begotten Son, c) that whosoever believeth in him should not perish, but have everlasting life.		
11.	Question	What does it say about God? (vs 16 a)
	Answer	
12.	Question	What did He do? 16 b)
	Answer	
13.	Question	Why did He do that? (vs 16 c)
	Answer	

1 Corinthians 13:4-8		
4 ¶ Love[22] suffers long, [and] is kind; love envies not; love vaunts[23] not itself, is not puffed up[24], 5 Does not behave itself unseemly, seeks not her own, is not easily provoked, thinks no evil; 6 Rejoices not in iniquity, but rejoices in the truth; 7 Bears all things, believeth all things, hopes all things, endures all things. 8 ¶ Love never fails: but whether [there be] prophecies, they shall fail; whether [there be] tongues, they shall cease; whether [there be] knowledge, it shall vanish away		
14.	Question	Write down 16 things this passage says about love.
	Answer	

---

[22] KJV uses the word charity. We substituted that word for a more modern word, which we understand, that word being "love".
[23] Does not brag.
[24] Is not proud.

Chapter 4   Kingdom Laws

		(Continue your answer here)

1 John 4:8		
8 He that loves not, knows not God; for God is love....		
15.	Question	What does this scripture say about love?
	Answer	

John 5:19		
19 a) Then answered Jesus and said unto them, Verily, verily, I say unto you, The Son can do nothing of himself, b) but what he sees the Father do: for what things so ever he does, these also do the Son likewise.		
16.	Question	What does Yeshua say about Himself in verse 19 a)?
	Answer	
17.	Question	Put in your own words what you think that statement meant?
	Answer	
18.	Question	What does Yeshua say about the things of the Father? (vs 9 b)

	Answer	
19.	Question	What do you think that statement meant?
	Answer	

Hebrews 9:14
14 a) How much more shall the blood of Christ, who through *the eternal Spirit* offered himself without spot to God …

20.	Question	Who does this verse say helped Yeshua offer Himself to God?
	Answer	

Genesis 1:1-2
1 ¶ In the beginning God created the heaven and the earth. 2 And the earth was without form, and void; and darkness was upon the face of the deep. *And the Spirit of God* moved upon the face of the waters.

21.	Question	What does this say about the Holy Spirit?
	Answer	

Galatians 6:24-25
24 And they that are Christ's have crucified the flesh with the affections and lusts. 25 If we live in the Spirit, let us also walk in the Spirit.

Chapter 4   Kingdom Laws

22.	Question	What has happened to those who are Messiah's? (vs 24)
	Answer	
23.	Question	What invitation does Paul, the author of Galatians, give to believers? (vs 25)
	Answer	

Galatians 5:22-23		
22 But the fruit of the Spirit is love, joy, peace, longsuffering[25], gentleness, goodness, faith, 23 Meekness, temperance[26]: against such there is no law."		
24.	Question	There are 9 things mentioned here that show the fruit of the Spirit. List those 9 things.
	Answer 1	
	2	
	3	
	4	
	5	
	6	

---

[25] Patience
[26] Self-control

Kingdom Keys for Kingdom Kids					Walking in Kingdom Power

		7	
		8	
		9	

1 Corinthians 12:4 to 13[27] lists the gifts of the Spirit. In the Box below and on the next page, these gifts are recapped. Read them and then move on to read the scripture following the box. Then answer the question.

THE GIFTS OF THE SPIRIT	
Message Gifts[28]	1. Prophecy
	2. Tongues[29]
	3. Interpretation of Tongues
Revelation Gifts	4. Word of Knowledge
	5. Word of Wisdom
	6. Discerning of spirits
Power Gifts	7. Miracles
	8. Healing
	9. Faith

1 Corinthians 14:12		
12 Even so ye, forasmuch as ye are zealous of spiritual gifts, seek that ye may excel to the edifying[30] of the church.		
25.	Question	Paul, the Apostle and author of 1 Corinthians writes about spiritual gifts. 2 Chapters earlier, he listed them. At this point, however, he relates that he desires believers to be zealous of spiritual gifts.

---

[27] Refer to your own Bible for these verses.
[28] Many say Gifts of Utterance
[29] While tongues are a gift of God whereby a person speaks in a language which they never before learned, this gift refers to an outward expression of tongues within a gathering, at which time, God speaks a message, which one with the gift of interpretation explains to all.
[30] To edify is to promote growth

Chapter 4   Kingdom Laws

		What reason does Paul give regarding the use of the gifts?
	Answer	

Romans 8:2		
2 For the law of the Spirit of life in Christ Jesus hath made me free from the law of sin and death.		
26.	Question	Name the two laws stated in this verse.
	Answer	
27.	Question	The first law mentioned in this verse did something. Write down what it did.
	Answer	

Romans 5:12		
12 a) Wherefore, as by one man sin entered into the world, and b) death by sin; and c) so death passed upon all men, d) for that all have sinned:"		
28.	Question	How did sin enter the world? (12 a)
	Answer	
29.	Question	What came in along with sin? (vs 12 b)
	Answer	

30.	Question	What happened to all men? (vs 12 c)
	Answer	
31.	Question	Why does that continue to happen? (vs 12 d)
	Answer	

Galatians 5:19-21
19 Now the works of the flesh are manifest, which are [these]; Adultery, fornication, uncleanness, lasciviousness, 20 Idolatry, witchcraft, hatred, variance, emulations, wrath, strife, seditions, heresies, 21 Envyings, murders, drunkenness, revellings, and such like: of the which I tell you before, as I have also told [you] in time past, that they which do such things shall not inherit the kingdom of God."

32.	Question	List the works of the flesh. (vs 19-21)	
	Answer		
33.	Question	This is a list of activities which Paul says the flesh manifest. Each one has a common denominator: "self". Read the list again with that thought in mind. Write, in the space below, whether you agree or	

Chapter 4 — Kingdom Laws

		disagree with the comment that self is the common denominator. Explain your reasons.
	Answer	
34.	Question	Verse 21 says that those who do such things will not inherit the Kingdom of God. Does that mean those things do not exist in God's Kingdom and therefore could not originate from there? Explain your answer.
	Answer	

Luke 4:18		
18 The Spirit of the Lord is upon me, because he hath anointed me to preach the gospel to the poor; he hath sent me to heal the brokenhearted, to preach deliverance to the captives, and recovering of sight to the blind, to set at liberty them that are bruised,		
35.	Question	As Yeshua preached the gospel, the Spirit of the Lord was upon Him. What signs accompanied His appointment to preach the gospel? (vs 18)

	Answer	

Acts 26:15-18
15 And I said, Who are you, Lord? And he said, I am Yeshua, whom you persecute. 16 But rise, and stand upon your feet: for I have appeared unto you for this purpose, to make you a minister and a witness both of these things which you have seen, and of those things in the which I will appear unto you; 17 Delivering you from the people, and from the Gentiles, unto whom now I send you, 18 *To open their eyes, and to turn them from darkness to light, and from the power of satan unto God, that they may receive forgiveness of sins, and inheritance among them which are sanctified by faith that is in me.*

36.	COMMENT	Prior to the conversion of the Apostle Paul, he persecuted the early, first century Christian believers. Yeshua confronted and turned him around. In the book of Acts, Luke, the physician, recapped the experience.
	Question	Verse 18 specifically outlines Paul's mission. Recap that mission in the space below.
	Answer	

Chapter 4		Kingdom Laws

Psalm 107:8-20		
8 Oh that men would praise YeHoVaH for his goodness, and for his wonderful works to the children of men! 9 For he satisfies the longing soul, and fills the hungry soul with goodness. 10 ¶ Such as sit in darkness and in the shadow of death, being bound in affliction and iron; 11 Because they rebelled against the words of God, and contemned the counsel of the most High: 12 Therefore he brought down their heart with labour; they fell down, and there was none to help. 13 Then they cried unto YeHoVaH in their trouble, and he saved them out of their distresses. 14 He brought them out of darkness and the shadow of death, and brake their bands in sunder. 15 Oh that men would praise YeHoVaH for his goodness, and for his wonderful works to the children of men! 16 For he has broken the gates of brass, and cut the bars of iron in sunder. 17 ¶ Fools because of their transgression, and because of their iniquities, are afflicted. 18 Their soul abhors all manner of meat; and they draw near unto the gates of death. 19 Then they cry unto YeHoVaH in their trouble, and he saves them out of their distresses. 20 He sent his word, and healed them, and delivered them from their destructions.		
37.	Comment	This scripture speaks of God's goodness to all humankind, both to those who do good and to those who do evil.
	Question	What happened to those who rebelled? (vs 10-12)
	Answer	

38.	Question	What happened after they cried out to God? (vs 13-18)
	Answer	
39.	Question	What happened after they cried out to God in verse 19? (include verse 20 in your answer)
	Answer	

40.	Look at the following chart entitled, Benefits of God's Kingdom. In the first column, there is a scripture. The second column is blank. Read the scripture and then recap, in the second column, the things that express **a benefit** of God's touch.

BENEFITS OF GOD'S KINGDOM	
Scripture	Characteristic
Isaiah 35: 5 Then the eyes of the blind shall be opened, and the ears of the deaf shall be unstopped.	
Psalm 146:8 YeHoVaH opens [the eyes of] the blind: YeHoVaH raises them that are bowed down: YeHoVaH loves the righteous:	
Matthew 11:5 The blind receive their sight, and the lame walk, the lepers are cleansed, and the deaf hear, the dead are raised up, and the poor have the gospel preached to them.	
Luke 24:45 Then opened he their understanding, that they might understand the scriptures,	
Acts 26:18 To open their eyes, [and] to turn [them] from darkness to light, and [from] the power of ha satan unto God, that they may receive forgiveness of sins, and inheritance among them which are sanctified by faith that is in me.	
2 Corinthians 4:6 For God, who commanded the light to shine out of darkness, hath shined in our hearts, to [give] the light of the knowledge of the glory of God in the face of Jesus Christ.	
Isaiah 9:2 The people that walked in darkness have seen a great light: they that dwell in the land of the shadow of death, upon them hath the light shined.	

A look at a few Hebrew root words:

Kingdom Keys for Kingdom Kids   Walking in Kingdom Power

As usual, turn to the Appendix. Look up the Hebrew word in its pictograph form. Recap its meaning in the spaces provided.

41.	Name
42.	Judgment
43.	Peculiar treasure

	(continue your answer here)
44.	Throne

45.	Dominion

PRECIOUS MOMENTS RECAP

46.	QUESTION:	Review this workbook chapter. Pick out the scriptures that spoke to you the most. Write at least one of those scriptures in the space below.

Chapter 4 — Kingdom Laws

	ANSWER:	
47..	QUESTION:	What specific truth from the scriptures you studied in this workbook chapter speaks to you. Write that truth in the space below.
	ANSWER:	

		(continue your answer here)
48.	QUESTION:	Think of how you can apply this scripture to your life. Enter those thoughts in the space below.
	ANSWER:	

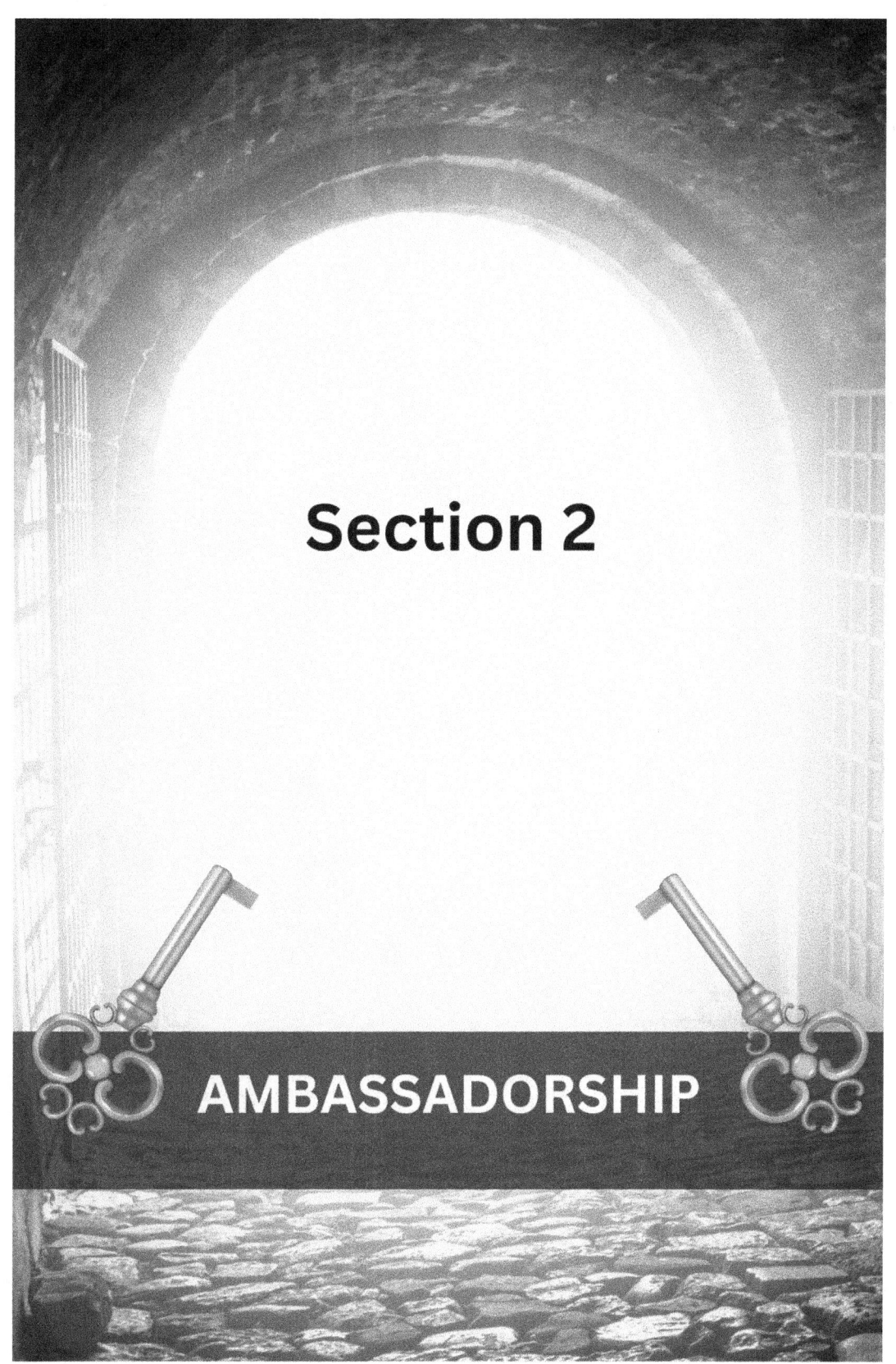

Section 2

AMBASSADORSHIP

KINGDOM INHERITANCE 5

REMEMBER:
- Begin with Prayer.
- Use the scripture in the workbook as a lesson of learning between you and your God!
- If you are not familiar with a certain passage, then go to your Bible and read some surrounding text.

Matthew 7:13-14			
13 Enter you in at the strait[31] gate: for wide is the gate, and broad is the way, that leads to destruction, and many there be which go in there at: 14 Because strait is the gate, and narrow is the way, which leads unto life, and few there be that find it.			
1.	Question	List the two types of gates mentioned in Matthew 7:13.	
	Answer	a	
		b	
2.	Question	Which way leads to eternal life? (vs 14)	
	Answer		
3.	Question	Why is the gate that leads to eternal life, described as "strait", and why do few people find it? Explain your answer.	
	Answer		

---

[31] Narrow

		Continue your answer here

Mathew 25:24		
34 Then shall the King say unto them on his right hand, Come, you blessed of my Father, inherit the kingdom prepared for you from the foundation of the world:		
4.	Question	According to verse 34, how does one get the Kingdom?
	Answer	
5.	Question	When was that kingdom prepared?
	Answer	
6.	Question	In the King's address, what does He call those that come?
	Answer	

1 Corinthians 15:50		
50 Now this I say, brethren, that flesh and blood cannot inherit the kingdom of God; neither does corruption inherit incorruption.		
7.	Question	List what this scripture says regarding those that will not inherit the kingdom.
	Answer	

Matthew 5:3		
3 Blessed [are] the poor in spirit: for theirs is the kingdom of heaven.[32]		
8.	Question	Who inherits the Kingdom of Heaven?
	Answer	

1 Corinthians 6:9		
9 Know you not that the unrighteous shall not inherit the kingdom of God?		
9.	Question	Who does not inherit the kingdom of God?
	Answer	

1 Corinthians 6:11		
11 a) And such were some of you: but you are washed, but you are sanctified, but you are justified in the name of the Lord Jesus, and b) by the Spirit of our God.		
10.	**COMMENT**	Between verse 9 and 11, the Apostle lists certain behaviours that some believers practiced earlier. Then he declares what they are now.
11.	Question	What 3 things does this scripture say regarding the present state of believers? (vs 11 a)
	Answer	

---

[32] Remember: the terms, "The Kingdom of God" and "The Kingdom of Heaven" are synonymous.

12.	Question	Who does this work? (vs 11 b)
	Answer	

Romans 9:8		
8 a) They, which are the children of the flesh, these are not the children of God: b) but the children of the promise are counted for the seed.		
13.	COMMENT	Children of the flesh, in the above scripture, refer to those Jewish believers who were of the seed of Abraham, in the flesh.
	Question	Is one a child of God by human birth? (vs 8 a) Circle the correct answer.
	Answer	Yes No
14.	Question	Who is a child of God? (vs 8 b)
	Answer	

Ephesians 1:12-14	
12 That we should be to the praise of his glory, who first trusted in Christ. 13 In whom you also trusted, after that you heard the word of truth, the gospel of your salvation: in whom also after that you believed, you were sealed with that holy Spirit of promise, 14 Which is the earnest[33] of our inheritance until the redemption of the purchased possession, unto the praise of his glory.	
15. Question	What did the people do in verse 12?
Answer	

---

[33] down payment

Chapter 5 — Kingdom Inheritance

16.	Question	When did they do this? (vs 13)
	Answer	
17.	Question	What happened after they believed? (vs 13)
	Answer	
18.	Question	How does verse 14 describe the happening in verse 13?
	Answer	

1 Corinthians 15:40-42

40 [There are] also celestial bodies, and bodies terrestrial: but the glory of the celestial [is] one, and the [glory] of the terrestrial [is] another. 41 [There is] one glory of the sun, and another glory of the moon, and another glory of the stars: for [one] star differeth from [another] star in glory. 42 So also is the resurrection of the dead. *It is sown in corruption; it is raised in incorruption:*

19.	Question	Name two bodies mentioned here? (vs 40)
	Answer	
20.	Question	Describe their glory. (vs 40)
	Answer	
21.	Question	Describe the specific bodies of the heavens in verse 41.
	Answer	
22.	Question	Are their glories the same? (vs 41) Yes or No answer is OK

	Answer	
23.	**COMMENT**	As these things are different so too is the resurrection. One is sown in corruption. This refers to the physical body. The other, Incorruption, refers to the spiritual man.
	Question	What does it mean to sow in corruption and be raised in incorruption? (vs 42)
	Answer	

John 5:25-29
25 Verily, verily, I say unto you, The hour is coming, and now is, when the dead shall hear the voice of the Son of God: and they that hear shall live. 26 For as the Father hath life in himself; so hath he given to the Son to have life in himself; 27 And hath given him authority <1849>[34] to execute judgment also, because he is the Son of man. 28 Marvel not at this: for the hour is coming, in the which all that are in the graves shall hear his voice, 29 And shall come forth; they that have done good, *unto the resurrection of life*; and they that have done evil, unto the resurrection of damnation.

24.	Question	What happens to the dead in verse 25?
	Answer	
25.	Question	What has the Father and Son according to verse 26?
	Answer	
26.	Question	What has the Father given Yeshua? (vs 27)
	Answer	
	Question	What is Yeshua to do with this? (vs 27)

---

[34] <1849.> is the # in Strong's Concordance for this Greek Word. The word means a "legal, judicial, deciding ability". It is like a judge that makes a decision, and that decision becomes law.

27.	Answer	
28.	Question	Why can Yeshua do this? (vs 27)
	Answer	
29.	Question	What is coming soon? (vs 28-29)
	Answer	

Matthew 6:27-34
27 Which of you by taking thought can add one cubit unto his stature? 28 And why take you thought for raiment? Consider the lilies of the field, how they grow; they toil not, neither do they spin: 29 And yet I say unto you, That even Solomon in all his glory was not arrayed like one of these. 30 Wherefore, if God so clothe the grass of the field, which today is, and tomorrow is cast into the oven, shall he not much more clothe you, O you of little faith? 31 Therefore take no thought, saying, What shall we eat? or, What shall we drink? or, Wherewithal shall we be clothed? 32 (For after all these things do the Gentiles seek:) for your heavenly Father knows that you have need of all these things. 33 But seek you first the kingdom of God, and his righteousness; and all these things shall be added unto you. 34 Take therefore no thought for the morrow: for the morrow shall take thought for the things of itself. Sufficient unto the day is the evil thereof.

30.	Question	What does this scripture tell believers to do? (vs 31 to 34)
	Answer	

Isaiah 55:9		
9 For as the heavens are higher than the earth, so are my ways higher than your ways, and my thoughts than your thoughts.		
	Question	What does it say about God's ways?

31.	Answer	
32.	Question	What does it say about God's thoughts?
	Answer	

1 Corinthians 2:16		
16 For who hath known the mind of the Lord, that he may instruct him? But we have the mind of Christ.		
33.	Question	What has God given to believers?
	Answer	
34.	Question	Does this mean, as a believer, you can know God's thoughts?
	Answer	
35.	Question	Can you give God counsel?
	Answer	

1 Corinthians 2:12-14		
12 Now we have received, not the spirit of the world, *but the spirit which is of God;* ³⁵that we might know the things that are freely given to us of God. 13 Which things also we speak, not in the words which man's wisdom teaches, but which the Holy Ghost teaches; comparing spiritual things with spiritual. 14 But the natural man receives not the things of the Spirit of God: for they are foolishness unto him: neither can he know them, because they are spiritually discerned.		
36.	Question	What spirit have believers received? (vs 12)
	Answer	

---

³⁵ Further shows the change of Spirit as in Point 1, and other places in this book.

37.	Question	Why do we have that spirit? (vs 12)
	Answer	
38.	Question	Paul, the author of this passage, says that he speaks of the things of God. How does he relate those things? (vs 13)
	Answer	
39.	Question	Who cannot receive the things of God? (vs 14)
	Answer	
40.	Question	Does this mean some can receive the things of the Spirit of God? (vs 14) Explain your answer.
	Answer	

Ephesians 1:19-23[36]
19 And what is the exceeding greatness of his power to us-ward who believe, according to the working of his mighty power, 20 Which he wrought in Christ, when he raised him from the dead, and set him at his own right hand in the heavenly places, 21 Far above all principality, and power, and might, and dominion, and every name that is named, not only in this world, but also in that which is to come: 22 And hath put all things under his feet, and gave him to be the head over all things to the church, 23 Which is his body, the fullness of him that fills all in all.

41.	Question	Where did God place Yeshua? (vs 20)
	Answer	
	Question	What is Yeshua above, as listed in verse 21- 22?

---

[36] You reviewed this in prayer format in Ephesians 1:15 to 23 in Chapter 1.

42.	Answer	

Ephesians 2:1-7
1 ¶ And you hath he quickened[37], who were dead in trespasses and sins; 2 Wherein in time past you walked according to the course of this world, according to the prince of the power of the air, the spirit that now works in the children of disobedience: 3 Among whom also we all had our conversation in times past in the lusts of our flesh, fulfilling the desires of the flesh and of the mind; and were by nature the children of wrath, even as others. 4 ¶ But God, who is rich in mercy, for his great love wherewith he loved us, 5 Even when we were dead in sins, hath quickened us together with Christ, (by grace you are saved;) 6 And hath raised us up together, and made us sit together in heavenly places in Christ Jesus: 7 That in the ages to come he might show the exceeding riches of his grace in his kindness toward us through Christ Jesus.

43.	Question	These verses refer to believers. Where did God place believers? (vs 6)
	Answer	
44.	Question	Why did God do that? (vs 7)
	Answer	

John 14:12
12 ¶ Verily, verily, I say unto you, He that believeth on me, the works that I do shall he do also; and greater works than these shall he do; because I go unto my Father.

---

[37] Made alive.

45.	Question	What can a person do who believes in Yeshua, according to verse 12?
	Answer	
46.	Question	Why is this possible? (vs 12)
	Answer	

John 14:13-17
13 And whatsoever you shall ask in my name, that will I do, that the Father may be glorified in the Son. 14 If you shall ask any thing in my name, I will do it. 15 ¶ If you love me, keep my commandments. 16 And I will pray[38] the Father, and he shall give you another Comforter, that he may abide with you forever; 17 Even the Spirit of truth; whom the world cannot receive, because it sees him not, neither knows him: but you know him; for he dwells with you, and shall be in you.

47.	Question	What happens when you ask for something in Yeshua's name? (vs 13-14)
	Answer	
48.	Question	What will we do if we love Yeshua? (vs 15)
	Answer	
49.	Question	What will Yeshua ask the Father? (vs 16)
	Answer	
50.	Question	Describe the Comforter's qualities outlined in verses 16-17.

---

[38] Ask

	Answer	
51.	Question	Where is this Comforter? (vs 17)
	Answer	

Luke 17:21
21 Neither shall they say, Lo here! or, lo there! for, behold, the kingdom of God is within you.

52.	Question	What does this say about the Kingdom of God?
	Answer	

PRECIOUS MOMENTS RECAP

53.	QUESTION:	Review this workbook chapter. Pick out the scriptures that spoke to you the most. Write at least one of those scriptures in the space below.
	ANSWER:	

Chapter 5　　　　　　　　　　　　　　　　　　Kingdom Inheritance

		Continue your answer here
54.	QUESTION:	What specific truth from the scriptures you studied in this workbook chapter speaks to you. Write that truth in the space below.
	ANSWER:	

55.	QUESTION:	Think of how you can apply this scripture to your life. Enter those thoughts in the space below.
	ANSWER:	

 KINGDOM AMBASSADORS   6

REMEMBER:
- Begin with Prayer.
- Use the scripture in the workbook as a lesson of learning between you and your God!
- If you are not familiar with a certain passage, then go to your Bible and read some surrounding text.

2 Corinthians 5:20		
20 Now then we[39] are ambassadors for Christ, as though God did beseech you by us: we pray you in Christ's stead, be you reconciled to God.		
1.	Question	What were the Apostles for Christ?
	Answer	
2.	Question	What did God do to those at Corinth through the Apostles?
	Answer	
3.	Question	What did Paul ask them?
	Answer	

---

[39] Paul refers to himself and those with him when they evangelized Corinth.

John 14:5-9		
5 Thomas said unto him, Lord, we know not whither you go; and how can we know the way? 6 Jesus said unto him, I am the way, the truth, and the life: no man cometh unto the Father, but by me. 7 If you had known me, you should have known my Father also: and from henceforth you know him, and have seen him. 8 Philip said unto him, Lord, show us the Father, and it suffices us. 9 Jesus said unto him, Have I been so long time with you, and yet have you not known me, Philip? he that has seen me hath seen the Father; and how say you then, Show us the Father?		
4.	Question	What did Yeshua say about Himself? (vs 6)
	Answer	
5.	Question	What did Yeshua say about Himself in verse 7?
	Answer	
6.	Question	What did Yeshua say about Himself in verse 9?
	Answer	

Hebrews 1:1-4		
1 ¶ God, who at sundry times and in divers manners spoke in time past unto the fathers by the prophets, 2 Has in these last days spoken unto us by his Son, whom he hath appointed heir of all things, by whom also he made the worlds; 3 Who being the brightness of his glory, and the express image of his person, and upholding all things by the word of his power, when he had by himself purged our sins, sat down on the right hand of the Majesty on high; 4 ¶ Being made so much better than the angels, as he hath by inheritance obtained a more excellent name than they.		
7.	Question	This passage speaks of Yeshua's excellence. What does verse 3 say about Yeshua?
	Answer	

| Chapter 6 | | Kingdom Ambassadors |

Psalm 16:11		
11 You will show me the path of life: in Your presence is fullness of joy; at your right hand there are pleasures for evermore.		
8.	Question	What will God show you?
	Answer	
9.	Question	What is in God's Presence?
	Answer	
10.	Question	What is at His Right Hand?
	Answer	

Romans 14:17		
17 For the kingdom of God is not meat and drink; but righteousness, and peace, and joy in the Holy Ghost.		
11.	Question	What is the kingdom of God not?
	Answer	
12.	Question	What is the kingdom of God?
	Answer	

Psalm 9:7
7 But YeHoVaH shall endure for ever: he hath prepared his throne for judgment. 8 a) And he shall judge the world in righteousness, b) he shall minister judgment to the people in uprightness.

13.	Question	Why has the Lord prepared His Throne? (vs 7)
	Answer	
14.	Question	What does verse 8 a) say He shall do?
	Answer	
15.	Question	How does God minister Judgment? (vs 8 b)
	Answer	

Romans 8:28		
28 And we know that all things work together for good to them that love God, to them who are the called according to his purpose.		
16.	Question	What does this say about "all things"?
	Answer	

Habakkuk 2:20		
20 But YeHoVaH is in his holy temple: let all the earth keep silence before him.		
17.	Question	Where is the Lord?
	Answer	
18.	Question	What should the earth do?
	Answer	
19.	Question	Why do you think this happens?
	Answer	

Psalm 103:19		
19 YeHoVaH hath prepared his throne <03678> in the heavens; and his kingdom rules over all.		
20.	Question	What does this say about God's throne?
	Answer	
21.	Question	What does it say about His Kingdom?
	Answer	

Psalm 47:8		
8 God reigns over the heathen: God sits upon the throne <03678> of his holiness.		
22.	Question	Who does God reign over?
	Answer	
23.	Question	What description does this give of God's throne?
	Answer	

Daniel 4:17		
17 This matter is by the decree of the watchers, and the demand by the word of the holy ones: to the intent that the living may know that the most High rules in the kingdom of men, and gives it to whomsoever he will, and sets up over it the basest (lowest) of men.		
24.	Question	What does it say about God regarding the Kingdom of men?
	Answer	

25.	Question	Who is in charge of those in power upon the earth?
	Answer	

2 Chronicles 16:9		
9 a For the eyes of YeHoVaH run to and fro throughout the whole earth, to show himself strong in the behalf of them whose heart is perfect toward him.		
26.	Question	What looks to and fro throughout the whole earth?
	Answer	
27.	Question	Why does that happen?
	Answer	
28.	Question	On whose behalf does He look?
	Answer	

1 Peter 3:12		
12 a For the eyes of the Lord are over the righteous, and his ears are open unto their prayers:		
29.	Question	Who does the Lord look at?
	Answer	
30.	Question	What does He listen for?
	Answer	

Chapter 6 — Kingdom Ambassadors

Romans 13:1		
1 Let every soul be subject unto the higher powers. For there is no power but of God: the powers that be are ordained of God.		
31.	**COMMENT**	"Higher powers" here refers to those in authority in governmental positions, people such as Kings, Governors, etc.
	Question	How do these powers come to be in power?
	Answer	
32. a	Question	Is there any authority in power that God does not put there?
	Answer	

1 Corinthians 2:7-9		
7 But we speak the wisdom of God in a mystery, even the hidden wisdom, which God ordained before the world unto our glory: 8 Which none of the princes of this world knew: for had they known it, they would not have crucified the Lord of glory. 9 But as it is written, Eye hath not seen, nor ear heard, neither have entered into the heart of man, the things which God hath prepared for them that love him. "But God hath revealed [them] unto us by his Spirit: for the Spirit searcheth all things, yea, the deep things of God.		
33.	Question	What does this scripture say about wisdom? (vs 7)
	Answer	
34.	Question	Do all people know this wisdom? (vs 8)
	Answer	

35.	Question	Can we know God's wisdom? (vs 9-10)
	Answer	

Psalm 145:10-13
10 ¶ All your works shall praise thee, O YeHoVaH; and your saints shall bless you. 11 They shall speak of the glory of your kingdom, and talk of your power; 12 To make known to the sons of men his mighty acts, and the glorious majesty of his kingdom. 13 Your kingdom is an everlasting kingdom, and Your dominion endures throughout all generations.

36.	Question	What will God's works do? (vs 10)
	Answer	
37.	Question	What do they speak about? (vs 11)
	Answer	
38.	Question	Why do they do this? (vs 12)
	Answer	
39.	Question	What does it say about God's Kingdom? (vs 13)
	Answer	

Go to the Appendix. Find the Word below and recap its meaning.

Chapter 6   Kingdom Ambassadors

40.	Ambassador

PRECIOUS MOMENTS RECAP

41.	QUESTION:	Review this workbook chapter. Pick out the scriptures that spoke to you the most. Write at least one of those scriptures in the space below.
	ANSWER:	

		Continue your answer here
42	QUESTION:	What specific truth from the scriptures you studied in this workbook chapter speaks to you. Write that truth in the space below.
	ANSWER:	

43.	QUESTION:	Think of how you can apply this scripture to your life. Enter those thoughts in the space below.
	ANSWER:	

KINGDOM GOVERNMENT   7

REMEMBER:
- Begin with Prayer.
- Use the scripture in the workbook as a lesson of learning between you and your God!
- If you are not familiar with a certain passage, then go to your Bible and read some surrounding text.

Acts 16:6-10
6 ¶ Now when they had gone throughout Phrygia and the region of Galatia, and *were forbidden of the Holy Ghost to preach the word in Asia*, 7 After they were come to Mysia, they assayed to go into Bithynia: *but the Spirit suffered them not.* 8 And they passing by Mysia came down to Troas. 9 And a vision appeared to Paul in the night; There stood a man of Macedonia, and prayed him, saying, Come over into Macedonia, and help us. 10 And after he had seen the vision, immediately we endeavoured to go into Macedonia, *assuredly gathering that the Lord had called us for to preach the gospel unto them.*

1.	Question	What did the Holy Ghost do? (vs 6-7)
	Answer	
2.	Question	What happened to Paul? (vs 9)
	Answer	
3.	Question	How did Paul respond? (vs 10)
	Answer	

115

Psalm 139:7-12
7 ¶ Whither shall I go from your spirit? or whither shall I flee from your presence? 8 If I ascend up into heaven, thou art there: if I make my bed in hell, behold, thou art there. 9 If I take the wings of the morning, and dwell in the uttermost parts of the sea; 10 Even there shall your hand lead me, and your right hand shall hold me. 11 If I say, Surely the darkness shall cover me; even the night shall be light about me. 12 Yea, the darkness hides not from thee; but the night shines as the day: the darkness and the light are both alike to thee.

4.	Comment	You did these verses earlier. As you read them here, think about the Psalmist and his relationship with God.	
	Question	Do you think such a relationship with God was possible under the First Covenant? Explain your reasoning using scripture. r	
	Answer		

Ephesians 6:11-12
11 Put on the whole armour of God, that you may be able to stand against the wiles of the devil. 12 For we wrestle not against flesh and blood, but against principalities, against powers, against the rulers of the darkness of this world, against spiritual wickedness in high places.

5.	Question	What do we wrestle? (vs 12)
	Answer	

Chapter 7   Kingdom Government

6.	Question	How do we protect ourselves? (vs 11)
	Answer	

Daniel 6:17-23
"**17** And a stone was brought, and laid upon the mouth of the den; and the king sealed it with his own signet, and with the signet of his lords; that the purpose might not be changed concerning Daniel. **18** ¶ Then the king went to his palace, and passed the night fasting: neither were instruments of musick brought before him: and his sleep went from him. **19** Then the king arose very early in the morning, and went in haste unto the den of lions. **20** And when he came to the den, he cried with a lamentable voice unto Daniel: *and* the king spake and said to Daniel, O Daniel, servant of the living God, is thy God, whom thou servest continually, able to deliver thee from the lions? **21** Then said Daniel unto the king, O king, live for ever. **22** My God hath sent his angel, and hath shut the lions' mouths, that they have not hurt me: forasmuch as before him innocency was found in me; and also before thee, O king, have I done no hurt. **23** Then was the king exceeding glad for him, and commanded that they should take Daniel up out of the den. So Daniel was taken up out of the den, and no manner of hurt was found upon him, because he believed in his God."

7.	Comment	If you are not familiar with this passage, be sure to go to your Bible and read some surrounding passages!
	Question	What was put at the mouth of the lion's den? (vs 17)
	Answer	
8.	Question	What did the king do and why? (vs 17)
	Answer	

9.	Question	What did the king do according to verse 18?
	Answer	
10.	Question	What did the king do according to verse 19?
	Answer	
11.	Question	What did the king do and say according to verse 20?
	Answer	
12.	Question	What did the king say according to verse 21?
	Answer	
15.	Question	How did Daniel respond? (vs 22)
	Answer	

Chapter 7   Kingdom Government

16.	Question	How did the king respond? (vs 23)
	Answer	

Ephesians 6:13-18
"**13** Wherefore take unto you the whole armour of God, that ye may be able to withstand in the evil day, and having done all, to stand. **14** Stand therefore, having your loins girt about with truth, and having on the breastplate of righteousness; **15** And your feet shod with the preparation of the gospel of peace; **16** Above all, taking the shield of faith, wherewith ye shall be able to quench all the fiery darts of the wicked. **17** And take the helmet of salvation, and the sword of the Spirit, which is the word of God: **18** Praying always with all prayer and supplication in the Spirit, and watching thereunto with all perseverance and supplication for all saints;"

17.	Question	What is one to take and why? (vs 13)
	Answer	

18.	Question	Once standing, what is one to do? (vs 14)
	Answer	

Kingdom Keys for Kingdom Kids — Walking in Kingdom Power

19.	Question	What is one to do according to verse 15?
	Answer	
20.	Question	What is one to do according to verse 16 and why?
	Answer	
21.	Question	What is one to do according to verse 17?
	Answer	
22.	Question	What is one to do according to verse 18?
	Answer	

Matthew 5:44		
"But I say unto you, Love your enemies, bless them that curse you, do good to them that hate you, and pray for them which despitefully use you, and persecute you;"		
23.	Question	What things does this verse tell us to do?

	Answer	

Psalm 45:6-7		
"**6** ¶ Thy throne, O God, *is* for ever and ever: the sceptre of thy kingdom *is* a right sceptre. **7** Thou lovest righteousness, and hatest wickedness: therefore God, thy God, hath anointed thee with the oil of gladness above thy fellows."		
24.	Question	What is the length of time God's throne operates? (vs 6)
	Answer	
25.	Question	What is the sceptre of His kingdom? (vs 6)
	Answer	
26.	Question	What does God love? (vs 7)
	Answer	
27.	Question	What does God hate? (vs 7)
	Answer	

28.	Question	What did God do because of these things? (vs 7)[40]
	Answer	

Psalm 89:14		
"Justice and judgment *are* the habitation of thy throne: mercy and truth shall go before thy face."		
29.	Question	What is the habitation of God's throne? [2 things]
	Answer	
30.	Question	What goes out before His face? [2 things]
	Answer	

Go to the Appendix. Find the Word below and recap its meaning.

31.	Watcher

---

[40] Note: This a prophetic word about Yeshua.

Chapter 7 — Kingdom Government

	(continue your answer here)

PRECIOUS MOMENTS RECAP

32.	QUESTION:		Review this workbook chapter. Pick out the scriptures that spoke to you the most. Write at least one of those scriptures in the space below.
	ANSWER:		
33.	QUESTION:		What specific truth from the scriptures you studied in this workbook chapter speaks to you. Write that truth in the space below.

	ANSWER:	
34.	QUESTION:	Think of how you can apply this scripture to your life. Enter those thoughts in the space below.
	ANSWER:	

		(continue your answer here)

ALL UNACCREDITED STUDENTS:

Go ahead and move on to the next section of the book.

ALL STUDENTS IN THE DEGREE PROGRAM

BEFORE MOVING ON, you must complete your reports and do your exam.

COURSE GRADING

This Grading applies to Courses 301 and 302, entitled, Kingdom Keys for Kingdom Kids.

SPECIFICS OF DEGREE GRADING	%
Online Course Audio Completion Acknowledgement............	7
Course Completion Acknowledgement.................................	2
Workbook Completion Acknowledgement...........................	5
Workbook Chapter Reviews	18
Section Review Form...	12
Personal Testimony of your spiritual benefit from the course...	8
All of the above must be submitted before scheduling the final exam	52
Online Course Final Exam...	48
TOTAL	100
Passing Grade to receive credits...	69
NOTE: Grade to continue taking courses for your degree	75

See the website for the forms to complete your reports.

COURSE 303

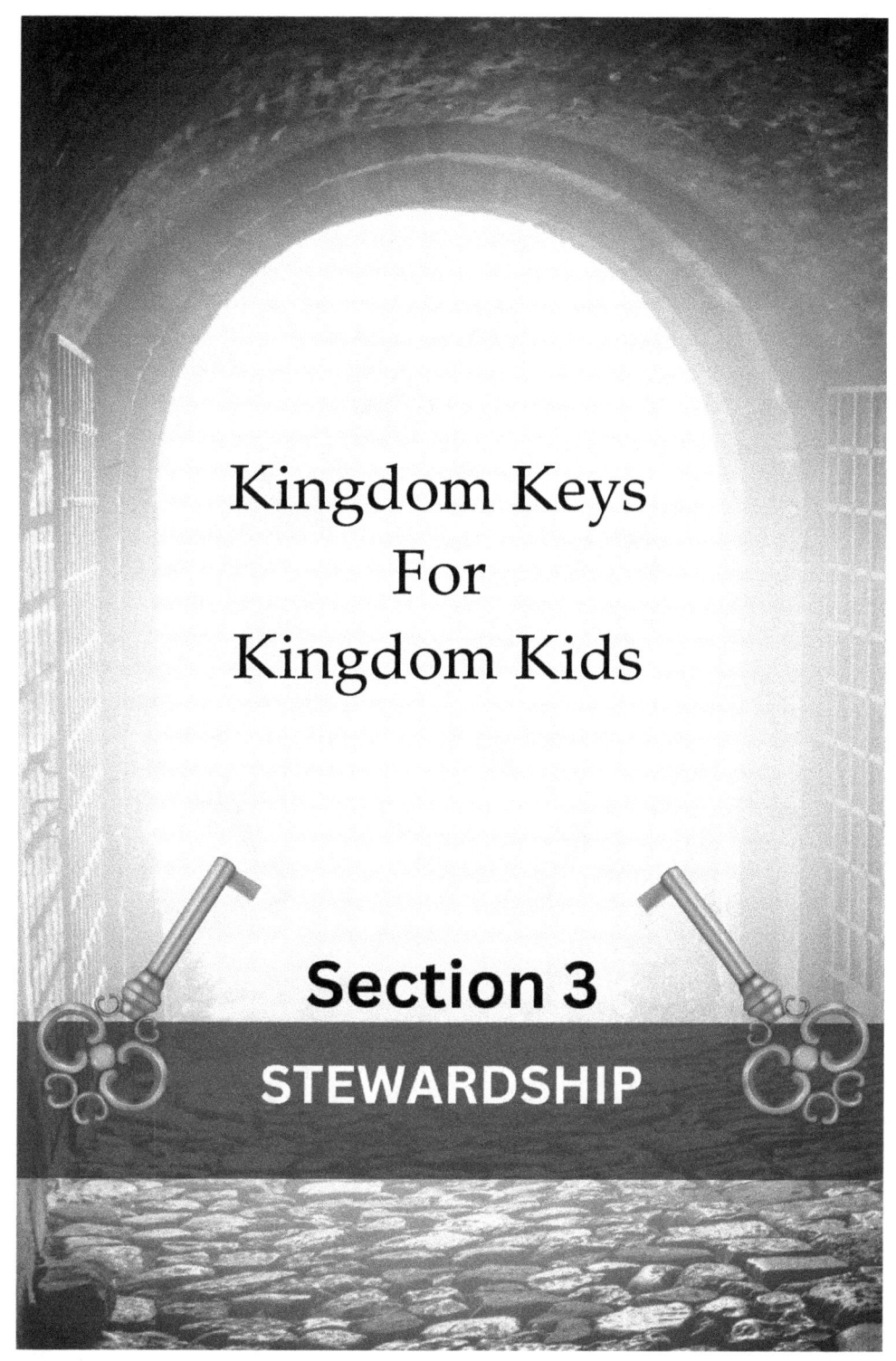

KINGDOM PRIORITIES   8

REMEMBER:
- Begin with Prayer.
- Use the scripture in the workbook as a lesson of learning between you and your God!
- If you are not familiar with a certain passage, then go to your Bible and read some surrounding text.

Luke 10:27			
27 And he answering said, You shall love the Lord your God with all your heart, and with all your soul, and with all your strength, and with all your mind; and your neighbour as yourself.			
1.	Comment	This scripture Yeshua gave, speaking of the first and greatest commandment.	
	Question	What are the priorities in a life given to God?	
	Answer		
2.	Question	Do you think this commandment still stands in place, today? Explain your reasoning with scripture.	
	Answer		

Exodus 19:5		
5 Now therefore, if ye will obey my voice indeed, and keep my covenant, then ye shall be a peculiar[41] treasure unto me *above all people*: for all the earth is mine:		
3.	Question	What does God consider a peculiar treasure?
	Answer	
4.	Question	What does it say about the owner of all the earth?
	Answer	

Deuteronomy 14:2		
2 For you are an holy people unto YeHoVaH your God, and YeHoVaH has chosen you to be a peculiar people unto himself, *above all the nations* that are upon the earth.		
5.	Question	What does it say here about a peculiar people?
	Answer	
6.	Question	What has God said regarding His Peculiar Treasure?
	Answer	

Matthew 21:42-44
42 Jesus saith unto them, Did ye never read in the scriptures, The stone which the builders rejected, the same is become the head of the corner[42]: this is the Lord's doing, and it is marvellous in our eyes? 43 Therefore say I unto you, The kingdom of God shall be taken from you, and given to a nation bringing

---

[41] Meaning a treasured people

[42] cornerstone

Chapter 8 — Kingdom Priorities

		forth the fruits thereof. 44 And whosoever shall fall on this stone shall be broken: but on whomsoever it shall fall, it will grind him to powder.
7.	Question	What did Yeshua say regarding the cornerstone? (vs 42)
	Answer	
8.	Question	What does it say about the Kingdom of God? (vs 43)
	Answer	
9.	Question	What happens to those who "fall on this stone"? (vs 44)
	Answer	
10.	Question	What happens to those upon whom this stone falls? (vs 44)
	Answer	

		1 Peter 1:15
		15 But as he which hath called you is holy, so be ye holy in all manner of conversation; Because it is written, Be ye holy; for I am holy.
11.	Question	God, who called us is Holy. Therefore, what should His people be like?
	Answer	

12.	Question	Explain, in your own words, what you think is meant by the word, "holy".
	Answer	

James 4:4
4 You adulterers and adulteresses, know you not that the friendship of the world is enmity with God? whosoever therefore will be a friend of the world is the enemy of God.

13.	Question	What does James call those who are friends with the world?
	Answer	
14.	Question	How does James see that friendship?
	Answer	
15.	Question	How does God see a friend of the world?
	Answer	
16.	Question	To what does the term "the world" refer?
	Answer	

1 Corinthians 29:10-13
10 ¶ Wherefore David blessed YeHoVaH before all the congregation: and David said, Blessed be thou, YeHoVaH God of Israel our father, for ever and ever. 11 Yours, O YeHoVaH, is the greatness, and the power, and the glory, and the victory, and the majesty: for all that is in the heaven and in the earth is Yours; yours is the kingdom, O YeHoVaH, and *You art exalted as head above all*. 12 Both riches and honour come of You, and You reign over all;

Chapter 8   Kingdom Priorities

and in Your hand is power and might; and in Your hand it is to make great, and to give strength unto all. 13 Now therefore, our God, we thank thee, and praise your glorious name.

17.	Question	What does David attribute to God in verse 11?
	Answer	
18.	Question	What does He attribute to God in verse 12?
	Answer	
19.	Question	How does this make David respond to God? (vs 13)
	Answer	

Matthew 6:13		
13 a) And lead us not into temptation, but deliver us from evil: b) For Yours is the kingdom, and the power, and the glory, for ever. Amen.		
20.	Question	What is the petition in verse 13 a)?
	Answer	
21.	Question	What is the statement in verse 13 b)?
	Answer	

Psalm 25:12-14
12 What man is he that fears YeHoVaH? him shall he teach in the way that he shall choose. 13 His soul shall dwell at ease; and his seed shall inherit the earth. 14 The secret of YeHoVaH is with them that fear him; and he will show them his covenant.

22.	Question	What and whom does God teach? (vs 12)
	Answer	
23.	Question	What shall his (man's) soul do? (vs 13)
	Answer	
24.	Question	What shall happen to his seed? (vs 13)
	Answer	
25.	Question	Where is the secret of the Lord? (vs 14)
	Answer	
26.	Question	What will God show them? (vs 14)
	Answer	

Psalm 37:9-11
9 For evildoers shall be cut off: but those that wait upon YeHoVaH, *they shall inherit the earth.* 10 For yet a little while, and the wicked shall not be: yea, you shall diligently consider his place, and it shall not be. 11 But the meek *shall inherit the earth*; and shall delight themselves in the abundance of peace.

27.	Question	What happens to those who do evil? (vs 9)
	Answer	
28.	Question	That happens to those that wait upon the Lord? (vs 9)
	Answer	

Chapter 8 	Kingdom Priorities

29.	Question	What happens to the meek? (vs 11)
	Answer	

2 Peter 1:2-4
"**2** Grace and peace be multiplied unto you through the knowledge of God, and of Jesus our Lord, **3** According as his divine power hath given unto us all things that *pertain* unto life and godliness, through the knowledge of him that hath called us to glory and virtue: **4** Whereby are given unto us exceeding great and precious promises: that by these ye might be partakers of the divine nature, having escaped the corruption that is in the world through lust."

30.	Question	How does Peter greet his listening audience? (vs 2)
	Answer	
31.	Question	What does verse 3 say about God's divine power?
	Answer	
32.	Question	What are we given and why, according to verse 4?
	Answer	
33.	Question	What have we escaped? (vs 4)
	Answer	

Leviticus 11:4		
"Nevertheless, these shall ye not eat of them that chew the cud, or of them that divide the hoof: *as* the camel, because he cheweth the cud, but divideth not the hoof; he *is* unclean unto you."		
34.	Question	What does this verse call unclean?
	Answer	
		The point here is that of separating between clean and unclean.

Psalm 37:4		
"Delight thyself also in YHVH; and he shall give thee the desires of thine heart."		
35.	Question	What does this scripture promise?
	Answer	
36.	Question	Is this promise conditional? If yes, describe the condition.
	Answer	

PRECIOUS MOMENTS RECAP

37..	QUESTION:	Review this workbook chapter. Pick out the scriptures that spoke to you the most. Write at least one of those scriptures in the space below.

Chapter 8 — Kingdom Priorities

	ANSWER:	
38.	QUESTION:	What specific truth from the scriptures you studied in this workbook chapter speaks to you. Write that truth in the space below.
	ANSWER:	

		(continue your answer here)
39.	QUESTION:	Think of how you can apply this scripture to your life. Enter those thoughts in the space below.
	ANSWER:	

KINGDOM BLESSINGS 9

- **REMEMBER:**
- Begin with Prayer.
- Use the scripture in the workbook as a lesson of learning between you and your God!
- If you are not familiar with a certain passage, then go to your Bible and read some surrounding text.

Romans 10:13		
13 For whosoever shall call upon the name of the Lord shall be saved.		
1.	Question	What happens to those who call upon the name of the Lord?
	Answer	
2.	Question	Describe the meaning of "whosoever".
	Answer	

Philippians 2:5-11
5 Let this mind be in you, which was also in Christ Jesus: 6 Who, being in the form of God, thought it not robbery to be equal with God: 7 But made himself of no reputation, and took upon him the form of a servant, and was made in the likeness of men: 8 And being found in fashion as a man, he humbled himself, and became obedient unto death, even the death of the

cross. 9 *Wherefore God also hath highly exalted him, and given him a name which is above every name:* 10 That at the name of Jesus every knee should bow, of things in heaven, and things in earth, and things under the earth; 11 And that every tongue should confess that Jesus Christ is Lord, to the glory of God the Father.

3.	Question	What mind is to be in believers? (vs 5)
	Answer	
4.	Question	Verse 6 to 8 speak of Yeshua's incarnation. Recap some comments on this subject. (vs 6 to 8)
	Answer	
5.	Question	What does verse 9 say God did to Yeshua?
	Answer	
6.	Question	What does verse 10 and 11 say about why God did this?
	Answer	

Nehemiah 9:5	
5 Then the Levites[43] said, Stand up and bless YeHoVaH your God for ever and ever: and blessed be thy glorious name, which is exalted above all blessing and praise.	
7.	Question	What did the Levites say about God's Name?

---

[43] 5 Jeshua, and Kadmiel, Bani, Hashabniah, Sherebiah, Hodijah, Shebaniah, and Pethahiah, declared the same thing.

Chapter 9   Kingdom Blessings

	Answer	

Deuteronomy 28:13, 45
UNDER THE FIRST COVENANT:
Obedience Results: Blessings: 13 And YeHoVaH shall make you the head, and not the tail; and you shall be above only, and you shall not be beneath; if that you hearken unto the commandments of YeHoVaH your God, which I command thee this day, to observe and to do them
Disobedience Results: Curses: 45 ¶ Moreover all these curses shall come upon you and shall pursue you, and overtake you, till you be destroyed ...

8.	**COMMENT**	Deuteronomy 28 is a lengthy chapter in which God outlines rewards for good behaviour and deterrents for bad. Rather than go through all the blessings and curses we only included the ones that sum up results of good or bad behaviour.
	Question	What happened under the First Covenant if you listened to God's commandments and carefully observed and did them? (vs 13)
	Answer	

143

9.	Question	Verse 45 applies to those disobedient to God's commandments. What is the end of such a person?
	Answer	

Isaiah 9:6		
6 For unto us a child[44] is born, unto us a son is given: and the government shall be upon his shoulder: and his name **[SHEM]**shall be called Wonderful, Counsellor, The mighty God, The everlasting Father, The Prince of Peace.		
10.	Question	What names (Shem) were given to the child?
	Answer	

Proverbs 21:22-24		
22 ¶ A wise man scales the city of the mighty, and casts down the strength of the confidence thereof. 23 ¶ Whoso keeps his mouth and his tongue keeps his soul from troubles. 24 ¶ *Proud and haughty scorner is his name, who deals in proud wrath.*		
11.	Question	What does verse 22 say a wise man does?
	Answer	
12.	Question	What does verse 23 say about a wise man?
	Answer	
13.	Question	What does 24 say about one who deals in proud wrath?

---

[44] This is reference to the Messiah.

	Answer	

Hebrews 13:8		
Hebrews 13:	8 Jesus Christ the same yesterday, and to day, and for ever.	
14.	Question	What does this say about Yeshua?
	Answer	

Hebrews 11:32-40
32 ¶ And what shall I more say? for the time would fail me to tell of Gedeon[45], and of Barak, and of Samson, and of Jephthae; of David also, and Samuel, and of the prophets: 33 Who *through faith* subdued kingdoms, wrought righteousness, obtained promises, stopped the mouths of lions, 34 Quenched the violence of fire, escaped the edge of the sword, out of weakness were made strong, waxed valiant in fight, turned to flight the armies of the aliens. 35 Women received their dead raised to life again: and others were tortured, not accepting deliverance; that they might obtain a better resurrection: 36 And others had trial of cruel mockings and scourgings, yea, moreover of bonds and imprisonment: 37 They were stoned, they were sawn asunder, were tempted, were slain with the sword: they wandered about in sheepskins and goatskins; being destitute, afflicted, tormented; 38 (Of whom the world was not worthy:) they wandered in deserts, and in mountains, and in dens and caves of the earth. 39 And these all, having obtained a good report *through faith*, received not the promise: 40 God having provided some better thing for us, that they without us should not be made perfect.

---

[45] Stories of Gideon, Barak, Samson, Jephthah are in the book of Judges.

15.	**COMMENT**	Verses 32 to 35 describe some believers who enjoyed great victory upon the earth. Verses 36 to 40 describe those who enjoyed a different kind of victory.
	Question	Both groups had a common factor. Describe that common factor and explain why it helped them to be victorious, even when in the face of death.
	Answer	

Chapter 9 — Kingdom Blessings

Ephesians 1:1-4		
"**1** Paul, an apostle of Jesus Christ by the will of God, to the saints which are at Ephesus, and to the faithful in Christ Jesus: **2** Grace *be* to you, and peace, from God our Father, and *from* the Lord Jesus Christ. "**3** ¶ Blessed *be* the God and Father of our Lord Jesus Christ, who hath blessed us with all spiritual blessings in heavenly *places* in Christ: **4** According as he hath chosen us in him before the foundation of the world[46], that we should be holy and without blame before him in love:"		
16.	Question	How does Paul greet the believers at Ephesus? (vs 1-2)
	Answer	
17.	Question	What does Paul say about blessings in verse 3?
	Answer	
18.	Question	When did God choose believers and why? (vs 4)
	Answer	

Deuteronomy 28:45		
"Moreover all these curses shall come upon thee, and shall pursue thee, and overtake thee, till thou be destroyed; because thou hearkenedst not unto the voice of YHVH thy God, to keep his commandments and his statutes which he commanded thee:"		
19.	Question	What does verse 45 say about curses?
	Answer	

---

[46] This speaks of God's foreknowledge of the future.

20.	Question	Why did these curses come upon the Israelites?
	Answer	

Romans 6:3-6			
"**3** Know ye not, that so many of us as were baptized into Jesus Christ were baptized into his death? **4** Therefore we are buried with him by baptism into death: that like as Christ was raised up from the dead by the glory of the Father, even so we also should walk in newness of life. **5** For if we have been planted together in the likeness of his death, we shall be also *in the likeness* of *his* resurrection: **6** Knowing this, that our old man is crucified with *him*, that the body of sin might be destroyed, that henceforth we should not serve sin."			
21.	Question	To what were believers baptized? (vs 3)	
	Answer		
22.	Question	To what were believers buried and why? (vs 4)	
	Answer		
23.	Question	Why did God do this, according to verse 5?	
	Answer		

Chapter 9 — Kingdom Blessings

24.	Question	What are we to know and why? (vs 6)
	Answer	

25. This is a very important scripture! Before leaving it, let us get a little creative! Let us draw out this scripture, putting ourselves in the picture.

a) Having been baptized into His death.

Take a stick figure to represent you and put yourself on the cross. Put a dove or a flame over your head to show the Holy Spirit baptizing you into Yeshua's death.

b) Buried with Him.

Take a stick figure to represent you and put yourself into the burial. Put a dove or a flame over your head to show the Holy Spirit baptizing you into Yeshua's burial.

c) Risen with Him

Take a stick figure to represent you with your hands lifted high and rejoicing. Put a dove or a flame over your head to show the Holy Spirit baptizing you into Yeshua's Resurrection.

Psalm 138:2		
"I will worship toward thy holy temple, and praise thy name for thy lovingkindness and for thy truth: for thou hast magnified thy word above all thy name."		
26.	Question	Why does the Psalmist praise God's name?
	Answer	

PRECIOUS MOMENTS RECAP

27.	QUESTION:	Review this workbook chapter. Pick out the scriptures that spoke to you the most. Write at least one of those scriptures in the space below.
	ANSWER:	

		(Continue your answer here)
28.	QUESTION:	What specific truth from the scriptures you studied in this workbook chapter speaks to you. Write that truth in the space below.
	ANSWER:	

29.	QUESTION:	Think of how you can apply this scripture to your life. Enter those thoughts in the space below.
	ANSWER:	

 KINGDOM AUTHORITY 10

- **REMEMBER:**
- **Begin with Prayer.**
- **Use the scripture in the workbook as a lesson of learning between you and your God!**
- **If you are not familiar with a certain passage, then go to your Bible and read some surrounding text.**

Matthew 21:43		
43 Therefore say I unto you, The kingdom of God shall be taken from you, and given to a nation bringing forth the fruits thereof.		
1.	Question	This passage records Yeshua's words to the leaders of the Jewish religion in His day. What did He tell them would happen to them?
	Answer	
2.	Question	What will God do with the Kingdom of God? Why?
	Answer	

3.	Question	How do you think that word applies to Gentile nations?
	Answer	

Ephesians 2:13-14		
13 But now in Christ Jesus you who sometimes were far off[47] are made nigh by the blood of Christ. 14 ¶ For he is our peace, who hath made both[48] one, and hath broken down the middle wall of partition between us;		
4.	Question	What happened to those who were earlier far off? (vs 13)
	Answer	
5.	Question	What is Messiah? (vs 14)
	Answer	
6.	Question	How did God make both Jew and Gentile one? (vs 14)
	Answer	

---

[47] "You who sometimes were far off" refers here to Gentiles. Gentiles were all other people groups other than Jews.
[48] Jew and Gentile

Chapter 10   Kingdom Authority

2 Peter 3:9		
9 a) The Lord is not slack concerning his promise, as some men count slackness; but is longsuffering to us-ward, b) not willing that any should perish, but that all should come to repentance.		
7.	Question	What is God towards humankind? (vs 9 a)
	Answer	
8.	Question	What is God's desire for all humankind? (vs 9 b)
	Answer	

Matthew 16:19		
19 And I will give unto you[49] the keys of the kingdom of heaven: and whatsoever you bind on earth shall be bound in heaven: and whatsoever you shall loose on earth shall be loosed in heaven.		
9.	Question	What does Yeshua say He gives? (vs 19)
	Answer	
10.	Question	What happens to what you bind?
	Answer	

---

[49] The person to whom Yeshua addressed was Peter. We will explain later on, but this verse applies to all believers.

11.	Question	What happens to what you loose?
	Answer	

Matthew 28:18-20		
"**18** And Jesus came and spake unto them, saying, All power is given unto me in heaven and in earth. **19** Go ye therefore, and teach all nations, baptizing them in the name of the Father, and of the Son, and of the Holy Ghost: **20** Teaching them to observe all things whatsoever I have commanded you: and, lo, I am with you alway, *even* unto the end of the world. Amen."		
12.	Question	What is given to Yeshua? (vs 18)
	Answer	
13.	Question	Define the parameters of the gift. (vs 18)
	Answer	
14.	Comment	The "therefore" ties verse 18 and 19 together.
	Question	What three things does Yeshua say to do because of verse 18? (vs 19)
	Answer	
15.	Question	What additional information does verse 20 give us regarding what we are to teach?
	Answer	

Chapter 10	Kingdom Authority

16.	Question	What promise does Yeshua give us? (vs 20)
	Answer	
17.	Question	Is this promise conditional? Explain your reasoning with scripture!
	Answer	

Hebrews 4:2-3		
2 For unto us was the gospel preached, as well as unto them: but the word preached did not profit them, not being mixed with faith in them that heard it. 3 For we which have believed do enter into rest, as he said, As I have sworn in my wrath, if they shall enter into my rest: although the works were finished from the foundation of the world.		
18.	**COMMENT**	This verse refers to the gospel message given to the church in the wilderness, that is the Jewish people under the leadership of Moses.
	Question	Why did the word they heard not profit them?
	Answer	

19.	Question	What happens to those who believe? (vs 3)
	Answer	
20.	Question	When did God do His work?
	Answer	

Revelation 13:7-8		
7 And it was given unto him[50] to make war with the saints, and to overcome them: and power was given him over all kindreds, and tongues, and nations. 8 And all that dwell upon the earth shall worship him, whose names are not written in the book of life of the ***Lamb slain from the foundation of the world***.		
21.	Question	What did the adversary do to the saints? (vs 7)
	Answer	
22.	Question	What was the purpose? (vs 7)
	Answer	
23.	Question	When was the Lamb of God slain? (vs 8)
	Answer	

Luke 24:49		
49 a) And, behold, I send the promise of my Father upon you: b) but tarry ye in the city of Jerusalem, until ye be endued with power from on high.		
24.	**COMMENT**	Yeshua spoke this to His disciples before His Ascension.

---

[50] This refers to the Beast mentioned in the Book of Revelation.

Chapter 10 — Kingdom Authority

	Question	What did Yeshua tell His disciples? (vs 49 a)
	Answer	
25.	Question	What were the disciples to do? (vs 49 b)
	Answer	
26.	Question	Why were they to do this? (vs 49 b)
	Answer	

Revelation 1:18

18 a) I am he that lives, and was dead; and, behold, I am alive for evermore, Amen; b) and have the keys of hell and of death.

27.	Question	What does Yeshua say about Himself? (vs 18 a)
	Answer	
28.	Question	What does Yeshua have? (vs 18 b)
	Answer	
29.	Question	What do you think is the significance of this ownership by Yeshua?
	Answer	

PRECIOUS MOMENTS RECAP

30.	QUESTION:	Review this workbook chapter. Pick out the scriptures that spoke to you the most. Write at least one of those scriptures in the space below.
	ANSWER:	
31.	QUESTION:	What specific truth from the scriptures you studied in this workbook chapter speaks to you. Write that truth in the space below.
	ANSWER:	

		(continue your answer here)
32.	QUESTION:	Think of how you can apply this scripture to your life. Enter those thoughts in the space below.
	ANSWER:	

		(continue your answer here)

KINGDOM KEYS   11

- **REMEMBER:**
- Begin with Prayer.
- Use the scripture in the workbook as a lesson of learning between you and your God!
- If you are not familiar with a certain passage, then go to your Bible and read some surrounding text.

Revelation 3:8		
8 a) I know thy works[51]: behold, I have set before thee an open door, b) and no man can shut it: c) for thou hast a little strength, and hast kept my word, and hast not denied my name.		
1.	Question	What has Yeshua set before His people? (vs 8 a)
	Answer	
2.	Question	How secure is that door? (vs 8 b)
	Answer	
3.	Question	What did that church do? (vs 8 c)
	Answer	

---

[51] This is Yeshua speaking to a church in the book of Revelation.

Mark 3:27		
27 a) No man can enter into a strong man's house, and spoil his goods, b) except he will first bind the strong man; and then he will spoil his house.		
4.	Question	Who can enter into a strong man's house and spoil his goods? (vs 27 a)
	Answer	
5.	Question	What makes it possible to enter the house? (vs 27 b)
	Answer	

John 16:33		
33 These things I[52] have spoken unto you, that in me ye might have peace. In the world ye shall have tribulation: but be of good cheer; I have overcome the world.		
6.	Question	What has Yeshua done for us?
	Answer	

1 John 5:4-5		
4 For whatsoever is born of God overcomes the world: and this is the victory that overcomes the world, even our faith. 5 Who is he that overcomes the world, but he that believeth that Jesus is the Son of God?		
7.	Question	Who overcomes the world? (vs 4)
	Answer	

---

[52] Yeshua spoke these words to His disciples when He was upon the earth.

8.	Question	What is the victory that overcomes the world? (vs 4)
	Answer	
9.	Question	Who overcomes the world? (vs 5)
	Answer	

Acts 8:37		
37 a) And Philip said, If you believe with all your heart, you may.		
10.	**COMMENT**	Philip spoke to an eunuch with whom he just shared the gospel. The man then asked Philip if he could be baptized. 37 a) gives Philip's answer.
11.	Question	What condition did Philip give to the man?
	Answer	

Below is a recap of the Greek Word Power. Please read it.

POWER	εξουσια pronounced ex-oo-see'-ah	**Strong's # 1849**
MEANING:		
This word indicates an ability to make legal decisions. It is the power of a person, whose very commands, to which others must submit and obey. For example, when a supreme court judge makes a decision in a legal case, where no appeal is possible, his decision stands firm. ***Thus, this word means the legal, judicial, deciding ability.***		

Refer again to the Appendix. Locate these two Hebrew words: Heart and Faith.

Recap their meaning in the appropriate boxes. Then answer the question that follow.

HEART[53]	לבב lay-bawb (or lev)	FAITH	אמונה em-oo-naw
Meaning:		Meaning:	
12.	What do these two words have in common? (You might not know the answer at this point. Don't fret if that is the case. You will discover the answer as you read the textbook.)		

---

[53] While there are a few Hebrew words translated as heart, and we need to look each up and view the context of the passage, a good general idea of heart is this word as it describes it most like Yeshua.

Chapter 11   Kingdom Keys

13. In this chapter, since the Bible study has not been too hard, we are going to do a mini chapter analysis. Begin by reading the following passage: Acts 10 & 11.

Acts 10:1-11:30
"**1** ¶ There was a certain man in Caesarea called Cornelius, a centurion of the band called the Italian *band*, **2** A devout *man*, and one that feared God with all his house, which gave much alms to the people, and prayed to God alway. **3** He saw in a vision evidently about the ninth hour of the day an angel of God coming in to him, and saying unto him, Cornelius. **4** And when he looked on him, he was afraid, and said, What is it, Lord? And he said unto him, Thy prayers and thine alms are come up for a memorial before God. **5** And now send men to Joppa, and call for *one* Simon, whose surname is Peter: **6** He lodgeth with one Simon a tanner, whose house is by the sea side: he shall tell thee what thou oughtest to do. **7** And when the angel which spake unto Cornelius was departed, he called two of his household servants, and a devout soldier of them that waited on him continually; **8** And when he had declared all *these* things unto them, he sent them to Joppa."   "**9** ¶ On the morrow, as they went on their journey, and drew nigh unto the city, Peter went up upon the housetop to pray about the sixth hour: **10** And he became very hungry, and would have eaten: but while they made ready, he fell into a trance, **11** And saw heaven opened, and a certain vessel descending unto him, as it had been a great sheet knit at the four corners, and let down to the earth: **12** Wherein were all manner of fourfooted beasts of the earth, and wild beasts, and creeping things, and fowls of the air. **13** And there came a voice to him, Rise, Peter; kill, and eat. **14** But Peter said, Not so, Lord; for I have never eaten any thing that is common or unclean. **15** And the voice *spake* unto him again the second time, What God hath cleansed, *that* call not thou common. **16** This was done thrice: and the vessel was received up again into heaven. **17** Now while Peter doubted in himself what this vision which he had seen should mean, behold, the men which were sent from Cornelius had made enquiry for Simon's house, and stood before the

gate, **18** And called, and asked whether Simon, which was surnamed Peter, were lodged there."

"**19** ¶ While Peter thought on the vision, the Spirit said unto him, Behold, three men seek thee. **20** Arise therefore, and get thee down, and go with them, doubting nothing: for I have sent them. **21** Then Peter went down to the men which were sent unto him from Cornelius; and said, Behold, I am he whom ye seek: what *is* the cause wherefore ye are come? **22** And they said, Cornelius the centurion, a just man, and one that feareth God, and of good report among all the nation of the Jews, was warned from God by an holy angel to send for thee into his house, and to hear words of thee. **23** Then called he them in, and lodged *them*. And on the morrow Peter went away with them, and certain brethren from Joppa accompanied him. **24** And the morrow after they entered into Caesarea. And Cornelius waited for them, and had called together his kinsmen and near friends. **25** And as Peter was coming in, Cornelius met him, and fell down at his feet, and worshipped *him*. **26** But Peter took him up, saying, Stand up; I myself also am a man. **27** And as he talked with him, he went in, and found many that were come together. **28** And he said unto them, Ye know how that it is an unlawful thing for a man that is a Jew to keep company, or come unto one of another nation; but God hath shewed me that I should not call any man common or unclean.

29 Therefore came I *unto you* without gainsaying, as soon as I was sent for: I ask therefore for what intent ye have sent for me? **30** And Cornelius said, Four days ago I was fasting until this hour; and at the ninth hour I prayed in my house, and, behold, a man stood before me in bright clothing, **31** And said, Cornelius, thy prayer is heard, and thine alms are had in remembrance in the sight of God. **32** Send therefore to Joppa, and call hither Simon, whose surname is Peter; he is lodged in the house of *one* Simon a tanner by the sea side: who, when he cometh, shall speak unto thee. **33** Immediately therefore I sent to thee; and thou hast well done that thou art come. Now therefore are we all here present before God, to hear all things that are commanded thee of God."

"**34** ¶ Then Peter opened *his* mouth, and said, Of a truth I perceive that God is no respecter of persons: **35** But in every nation he that feareth him, and worketh righteousness, is accepted with him. **36** The word which *God* sent unto the children of Israel, preaching peace by Jesus Christ: (he is Lord of all:) **37** That word, *I say*, ye know, which was published throughout all Judaea, and began from Galilee, after the baptism which John preached; **38** How God anointed Jesus of Nazareth with the Holy Ghost and with power: who went about doing good, and healing all that were oppressed of the devil; for God was with him. **39** And we are witnesses of all things which he did both in the land of the Jews, and in Jerusalem; whom they slew and hanged on a tree: **40** Him God raised up the third day, and shewed him openly;

41 Not to all the people, but unto witnesses chosen before of God, *even* to us, who did eat and drink with him after he rose from the dead. **42** And he commanded us to preach unto the people, and to testify that it is he which was ordained of God *to be* the Judge of quick and dead. **43** To him give all the prophets witness, that through his name whosoever believeth in him shall receive remission of sins."

"**44** ¶ While Peter yet spake these words, the Holy Ghost fell on all them which heard the word. **45** And they of the circumcision which believed were astonished, as many as came with Peter, because that on the Gentiles also was poured out the gift of the Holy Ghost. **46** For they heard them speak with tongues, and magnify God. Then answered Peter, **47** Can any man forbid water, that these should not be baptized, which have received the Holy Ghost as well as we? **48** And he commanded them to be baptized in the name of the Lord. Then prayed they him to tarry certain days."

"**11:1** ¶ And the apostles and brethren that were in Judaea heard that the Gentiles had also received the word of God. **2** And when Peter was come up to Jerusalem, they that were of the circumcision contended with him, **3** Saying, Thou wentest in to men uncircumcised, and didst eat with them. **4** But Peter rehearsed *the matter* from the beginning, and expounded *it* by order unto them, saying, **5** I was in the city of Joppa praying: and in a trance I saw a vision, A certain vessel descend, as it had been a great sheet, let down from heaven by four corners; and it came even to me: **6** Upon the which when I had fastened mine eyes, I considered, and saw fourfooted beasts of the earth, and wild beasts, and creeping things, and fowls of the air. **7** And I heard a voice saying unto me, Arise, Peter; slay and eat. **8** But I said, Not so, Lord: for nothing common or unclean hath at any time entered into my mouth. **9** But the voice answered me again from heaven, What God hath cleansed, *that* call not thou common. **10** And this was done three times: and all were drawn up again into heaven.

11 And, behold, immediately there were three men already come unto the house where I was, sent from Caesarea unto me. **12** And the Spirit bade me go with them, nothing doubting. Moreover these six brethren accompanied me, and we entered into the man's house: **13** And he shewed us how he had seen an angel in his house, which stood and said unto him, Send men to Joppa, and call for Simon, whose surname is Peter; **14** Who shall tell thee words, whereby thou and all thy house shall be saved. **15** And as I began to speak, the Holy Ghost fell on them, as on us at the beginning. **16** Then remembered I the word of the Lord, how that he said, John indeed baptized with water; but ye shall be baptized with the Holy Ghost. **17** Forasmuch then as God gave them the like gift as *he did* unto us, who believed on the Lord Jesus Christ; what was I, that I could withstand God? **18** When they heard these things, they held their peace, and glorified God, saying, Then hath God also to the Gentiles granted repentance unto life."

"**19** ¶ Now they which were scattered abroad upon the persecution that arose about Stephen travelled as far as Phenice, and Cyprus, and Antioch, preaching the word to none but unto the Jews only. **20** And some of them were men of Cyprus and Cyrene, which, when they were come to Antioch, spake unto the Grecians, preaching the Lord Jesus. **21** And the hand of the Lord was with them: and a great number believed, and turned unto the Lord. **22** Then tidings of these things came unto the ears of the church which was in Jerusalem: and they sent forth Barnabas, that he should go as far as

> Antioch. **23** Who, when he came, and had seen the grace of God, was glad, and exhorted them all, that with purpose of heart they would cleave unto the Lord. **24** For he was a good man, and full of the Holy Ghost and of faith: and much people was added unto the Lord. **25** Then departed Barnabas to Tarsus, for to seek Saul: **26** And when he had found him, he brought him unto Antioch. And it came to pass, that a whole year they assembled themselves with the church, and taught much people. And the disciples were called Christians first in Antioch."
>
> "**27** ¶ And in these days came prophets from Jerusalem unto Antioch. **28** And there stood up one of them named Agabus, and signified by the Spirit that there should be great dearth throughout all the world: which came to pass in the days of Claudius Caesar. **29** Then the disciples, every man according to his ability, determined to send relief unto the brethren which dwelt in Judaea: **30** Which also they did, and sent it to the elders by the hands of Barnabas and Saul."

Next, take some coloured pencils and highlight any references to God, Holy Spirit (Ghost), or Yeshua (Jesus).

13. In the space below, recap the occurrences of the Godhead, stating what happened. Be sure to give the verse reference! Use loose leaf paper if you need more space.

Father (God)	

Son (often Lord)	
Holy Spirit	

14.. a) Next, take some additional coloured pencils and highlight any references to others, such as angels, people. .
b) List all those involved. (Try and find at least 10!)

1

2

3

4

5

6

7

8

9

10

11

12

15. Next, recap the vision given to Cornelius. *(Note: it is recorded more than once, so be sure you get all the information.)*

(continue your answer here)

16. Next, recap the vision given to Peter. *(Note: it is recorded more than once, so be sure you get all the information.)*

(continue your answer here)

That's enough of an analysis at this time!

PRECIOUS MOMENTS RECAP

17.	QUESTION	Review this workbook chapter. Pick out the scriptures that spoke to you the most. Write at least one of those scriptures in the space below.
	ANSWER	

		Continue your answer here
18.	QUESTION:	What specific truth from the scriptures you studied in this workbook chapter speaks to you. Write that truth in the space below.
	ANSWER:	

19.	QUESTION:	Think of how you can apply this scripture to your life. Enter those thoughts in the space below.
	ANSWER:	

KINGDOM TREASURES 12

(The Conclusion is included in this section.)

- **REMEMBER:**
- Begin with Prayer.
- Use the scripture in the workbook as a lesson of learning between you and your God!
- If you are not familiar with a certain passage, then go to your Bible and read some surrounding text.

Matthew 6:17-18		
17 But you, when you fast, anoint your head, and wash your face; 18 That you appear not unto men to fast, but unto your Father which is in secret: and your Father, which sees in secret, shall reward you openly. -		
1.	Question	What is one to do when they fast? (vs 17)
	Answer	
2.	Question	What is the reason for doing so? (vs 18)
	Answer	
3.	Question	What does the Father do?
	Answer	

Isaiah 29:13		
13 a) Wherefore the Lord said, Forasmuch as this people draw near me with their mouth, and with their lips do honour me, b) but have removed their heart far from me, c) and their fear toward me is taught by the precept of men:		
4.	Question	What do the people do here? (vs 13 a)
	Answer	
5.	Question	Where is the people's heart? (vs 13 b)
	Answer	
6.	Question	From where did their fear of God come? (vs 13 c)
	Answer	

Mark 12:41-44		
41 ¶ And Jesus sat over against the treasury, and beheld how the people cast money into the treasury: and many that were rich cast in much. 42 And there came a certain poor widow, and she threw in two mites, which make a farthing. 43 And he called unto him his disciples, and said unto them, Verily I say unto you, That this poor widow hath cast more in, than all they which have cast into the treasury: 44 For all they did cast in of their abundance; but she of her want did cast in all that she had, even all her living.		
7.	Question	Yeshua watched as the people brought their offering to God. What did the widow do?
	Answer	
8.	Question	What did Yeshua say about her gift? (vs 43-44)
	Answer	

Chapter 12   Kingdom Treasures

9.	Question	What lesson could we learn from this widow?
	Answer	

Matthew 6:19-21
19 [54] Lay not up for yourselves treasures upon earth, where moth and rust doth corrupt, and where thieves break through and steal: 20 But lay up for yourselves treasures in heaven, where neither moth nor rust doth corrupt, and where thieves do not break through nor steal: 21 For where your treasure is, there will your heart be also.

10.	Question	What advice did Yeshua give here? (vs 19-21)
	Answer	

11.	Question	What do you think must happen before a person lives as Yeshua suggested.
	Answer	

Luke 9:12-17
12 And when the day began to wear away, then came the twelve, and said unto him, Send the multitude away, that they may go into the towns and country round about, and lodge, and get victuals[55]: for we are here in a desert

---

[54] Yeshua speaks here to His disciples.
[55] food

place[56]. 13 But he said unto them, Give ye them to eat. And they said, We have no more but five loaves and two fishes; except we should go and buy meat for all this people. 14 For they were about five thousand men. And he said to his disciples, Make them sit down by fifties in a company. 15 And they did so, and made them all sit down. 16 Then he took the five loaves and the two fishes, and looking up to heaven, he blessed them, and brake, and gave to the disciples to set before the multitude. 17 And they did eat, and were all filled: and there was taken up of fragments that remained to them twelve baskets.

12.	Question	Recap this scripture in the space below.
	Answer	
13.	Question	Why do you think Yeshua did this miracle?
	Answer	

John 6:26-27
26 Jesus answered them and said, Verily, verily, I say unto you, Ye seek me, not because ye saw the miracles, but because ye did *eat of the loaves, and were filled.* 27 Labour not for the meat which perishes, but for that meat *which endures unto everlasting life,* which the Son of man shall give unto you: for him hath God the Father sealed.

	Question	What does Yeshua say in this scripture?

---

[56] No food available in that place

Chapter 12 — Kingdom Treasures

14.	Answer	

Matthew 14:22-33

22 And straightway Jesus constrained his disciples to get into a ship, and to go before him unto the other side, while he sent the multitudes away. 23 And when he had sent the multitudes away, he went up into a mountain apart to pray: and when the evening was come, he was there alone. 24 But the ship was now in the midst of the sea, tossed with waves: for the wind was contrary. 25 And in the fourth watch of the night Jesus went unto them, walking on the sea. 26 And when the disciples saw him walking on the sea, they were troubled, saying, It is a spirit; and they cried out for fear. 27 But straightway Jesus spoke unto them, saying, Be of good cheer; it is I; be not afraid. 28 And Peter answered him and said, Lord, if it be thou, bid me come unto thee on the water. 29 And he said, Come. And when Peter was come down out of the ship, he walked on the water, to go to Jesus. 30 But when he saw the wind boisterous, he was afraid; and beginning to sink, he cried, saying, Lord, save me. 31 And immediately Jesus stretched forth his hand, and caught him, and said unto him, O thou of little faith, wherefore didst thou doubt? 32 And when they were come into the ship, the wind ceased. 33 Then they that were in the ship came and worshipped him, saying, Of a truth thou art the Son of God..

15.	Question	Recap what happened in this scripture.
	Answer	

16.	Question	Why do you think Yeshua performed this miracle?
	Answer	

John 6:18-21
18 And the sea arose by reason of a great wind that blew. 19 So when they had rowed about five and twenty or thirty furlongs, they see Jesus walking on the sea, and drawing nigh unto the ship: and they were afraid. 20 But he said unto them, It is I; be not afraid. 21 Then they willingly received him into the ship: and immediately the ship was at the land whither they went.

17.	Question	This is another account of the same story as above. This one however, speaks of a miracle regarding the ship. Write down the miracle.
	Answer	
18.	Question	Why do you think Yeshua performed this miracle?
	Answer	

John 5:2-9
2 Now there is at Jerusalem by the sheep market a pool, which is called in the Hebrew tongue Bethesda, having five porches. 3 In these lay a great

multitude of impotent folk, of blind, halt, withered, waiting for the moving of the water. 4 For an angel went down at a certain season into the pool, and troubled the water: whosoever then first after the troubling of the water stepped in was made whole of whatsoever disease he had.

5 And a certain man was there, which had an infirmity thirty and eight years. 6 When Jesus saw him lie, and knew that he had been now a long time in that case, he said unto him, Wilt thou be made whole? 7 The impotent man answered him, Sir, I have no man, when the water is troubled, to put me into the pool: but while I am coming, another steps down before me. 8 Jesus said unto him, Rise, take up thy bed, and walk. 9 And immediately the man was made whole, and took up his bed, and walked: and on the same day was the Sabbath.

19.	Question	Recap this miracle.
	Answer	
20.	Question	Why do you think Yeshua performed this miracle?
	Answer	

Galatians 4:9		
9 But now, after that ye have known God, or rather are known of God, how turn ye again to the weak and beggarly elements, whereunto ye desire again to be in bondage.		
21.	Question	What question is asked here?
	Answer	
22.	Question	What does turning to these elements bring?
	Answer	
23.	Question	Name some things Paul might have considered "weak and beggarly elements". (Hint: remember Paul spoke to those who wanted to live under the Law and not Grace.)
	Answer	

Hebrews 6:1-2
1 Therefore leaving the principles of the doctrine of Christ, let us go on unto perfection; not laying again the foundation of repentance from dead works, and of faith toward God, 2 Of the doctrine of baptisms, and of laying on of hands, and of resurrection of the dead, and of eternal judgment.

24.	Question	What does the author of Hebrews command we leave behind? (vs 1)
	Answer	

25.	Question	What are some of those principles? (vs 1 and 2)
	Answer	

Acts 1:1-3
1 ¶ The former treatise have I made, O Theophilus, of all that Jesus began both to do and teach, 2 Until the day in which he was taken up, after that he through the Holy Ghost had given commandments unto the apostles whom he had chosen: 3 To whom also he showed himself alive after his passion by many infallible proofs, being seen of them forty days, and speaking of the things pertaining to the kingdom of God.

26.	Question	Yeshua spoke to His disciples after His Death. According to Acts 1:3, of what did He speak? (vs 3)
	Answer	

27. In the Appendix of the textbook, there is a message of Salvation. Below, we have-written a check list. Please read it and check off that to which you agree.

I.	Yeshua was a person who never sinned	
II.	God, for every human being on the earth, made Yeshua become sin, in His Eyes, so that He might pay the penalty for sin.	
III.	Yeshua paid that penalty. He died on the cross and was buried in a tomb.	
IV.	Three days later, He rose again, appearing to His disciples to show them the reality of His resurrection.	
V.	Yeshua could not stay in the tomb because "death" comes to all who sin, but since Yeshua never sinned, death could not hold Him in the grave.	
VI.	All those who come to Yeshua to receive Him as their Saviour, receive liberty from sin and from its horrible consequence, eternal death.	
VII.	They enter God's Kingdom and receive eternal life as well as another gift: the Righteousness of Messiah's life. After salvation, when God looks at the believer, He sees Yeshua's perfect life and sees a redeemed believer, set aside for God, and now that took place, the Holy Spirit dwells within them.	
VIII.	All it takes to receive this from God, is repentance for sinning against God and against man [57] and faith to receive His gift of Salvation.	

---

[57] When a person steals, etc. they sin against both God and man,

Chapter 12   Kingdom Treasures

PRECIOUS MOMENTS RECAP

28.	QUESTION:	Review this workbook chapter. Pick out the scriptures that spoke to you the most. Write at least one of those scriptures in the space below.
	ANSWER:	
29.	QUESTION:	What specific truth from the scriptures you studied in this workbook chapter speaks to you. Write that truth in the space below.

	ANSWER:	
30.	QUESTION:	Think of how you can apply this scripture to your life. Enter those thoughts in the space below.
	ANSWER:	

TO STUDENTS IN THE DEGREE PROGRAM

COURSE GRADING

This Grading applies to Courses 302 and 303,
entitled, Kingdom Keys for Kingdom Kids

SPECIFICS OF DEGREE GRADING	%
Online Course Audio Completion Acknowledgement...............	7
Course Completion Acknowledgement.................................	2
Workbook Completion Acknowledgement...........................	5
Workbook Chapter Reviews	18
Section Review Form...	12
Personal Testimony of your spiritual benefit from the course......	8
All of the above must be submitted before scheduling the final exam	**52**
Online Course Final Exam...	48
TOTAL	100
Passing Grade to receive credits...	69
NOTE: Grade to continue taking courses for your degree	**75**

APPENDIX

HEBREW WORD PICTURE MEANINGS

Remember, the following pages contain *possible meanings* of Hebraic Word Pictures! Do not treat them as hard and fast definitions! Also, some of these meanings, you may have read before in other courses. Definitions may be similar but not identical, as greater insight often comes with experience, over time.

AMBASSADOR	pronounced	Strongs # Hebrew
צִיר	tziyr tseer	6735

Parent Root:		
צ	tsade	(a person asleep on their side), a person resting, or in a position of rest
י	yod	(an arm stretched out) Work or deeds done
Picture		A person resting in a position from which they operate or do their work

Child Root:		
ר	resh	(a head), first, above, highest, supreme, top of, beginning of, top, first position, rule
Picture		Above, leader

WHOLE PICTURE: In this case, the word picture shows someone in a position from which they operate, with a special authority given to them which puts them above others in the country of visitation.

COMMENTS: Looking at the word, in that light, an ambassador works from an authoritative position. In addition, an ambassador both negotiates and represents their homeland. When people look at the ambassador they should see a reflection of the country from where the ambassador originates. With the thought in mind think how others see God's ambassadors (believers) and should experience the Kingdom of God which they represent and present a message.

NOTE: THERE ARE OTHER WORDS FOR AMBASSADOR. Some imply a special delegation for a one-time visit.

BLESS [58]			pronounced	Strongs # Hebrew
ברך			baw-rak'	1288
Parent Root:				
ב	bet		(house) In this instance, consider this as a person's vessel (their body).	
ר	resh		(head) In this instance, consider this something high or above as the head is above the shoulder.	
Picture			The person is above, the highest	
Child Root:				
ך	kaf		(hand) Consider this as a hand, ready to give something away. Look at it as a representation of Divine power, giving limitlessly, without restraint.	
Picture			Unrestrained	
WHOLE PICTURE:			Man (the person) is the 'highest', or supreme being without restraint upon the earth. Man is to be higher than all that he encounters, in that sense; he is to have limitless rulership.	
COMMENTS:			Just one more evidence that God set man 'to be the head and not the tail', to be above everything, situation, etc. that he/she encountered in life.	
PLEASE NOTE: In the picture of the house and head and hand, we see that a blessing positions a person to rise above whatever opposes them. A further understanding shows that it is by God's Divine power that all opposition stops and a person rises above their circumstances.				

---

[58] While the base of letter meanings refer to Dr. Seekins teachings, the Hebrew words presented in this workbook *as well as the word's possible original meaning, come from the author's own work.*

CURSE	pronounced	Strongs # Hebrew
ארר	aw-rar'	0779

Parent Root:

א	aleph	(ox) In this instance, consider this as something strong, powerful, leading.
ר	resh	(head) In this instance, consider something that is at the top in a position to rule.

Pulling strength, which becomes supreme.

Child Root:

ר	resh	(head) In this instance, consider something at the top, above other things.
Picture		Rules, ruling

PICTURE: A curse is something that establishes itself as "supreme" over a person's life and then "rules" that person.

COMMENT: when God cursed the ground in Genesis 4: 9, the ground would not easily produce crops, but rather it would easily produce weeds, thorns, and thistles. That aspect of wild growth became dominant over the ground. The "wild" aspect of the earth only came to be when God cursed the ground for man's sake.

Please note: When a person is cursed, whatever comes against them, rules over them. (God did not curse man in the garden! He cursed *the ground* on behalf of man so that man would look to God for what he needed.)

DOMINION[59]	pronounced	Strongs # Hebrew
רדה	"raw daw"	7287
Parent Root:		
ר	resh	(head) In this instance, above all, supreme or overcoming.
ד	dalet	(door) In this instance, doorways such as situations.
Picture		Above all situations or incidents.
Child Root:		
ה	heh	In this instance, greatly rejoicing.
Picture		Rejoicing.
WHOLE PICTURE:		Head over all events, circumstances, etc. rejoicing as an overcomer.
COMMENTS:		Adam was created to be "above" every circumstance on the earth, no matter what he might encounter. God made that possible.
Please Note:		This word carries with it the idea of ruling over and above that which comes against you.

---

[59] This is one of several words for Dominion. This one comes from Genesis 1:28

FAITH[60] אמונה	pronounced "em-oo-naw"	Strongs # Hebrew 0530
א	aleph	(Ox) In this instance, a strong pull or leading.
מ	mem	(waves) In this instance, matters of life, things that move one along like waves of the sea.
Parent Root		
Picture		The strong guide or pull in the matters of life
Child Root:		
ו	vav	(nail) In this instance, to come along side to help a person
נ	nun	(seed of life) In this instance, birthing of activities.
ה	heh	(man with hands above head) In this instance, to surrender or give up, and/or awesome.
Picture:		Coming along side to help birth activities which bring surrender and or awesome results.
OVERAL PICTURE		Faith is a strong, drawing type of leadership, helping one to overcome life's issues, and as such, it attaches itself to a person to bring all works and deeds to complete surrender to follow its leadership which outcome is nothing short of awesome.
COMMENT:		One who has faith is one who has the strength of leadership, overcoming, in all areas of life and its works or activities going on within those issues of life. The leadership is secure, and one surrenders to it.

---

[60] There are many words for FAITH. This word comes from Habakkuk 2:4, "the just shall live by faith".

HEART[61]	pronounced	Strongs # Hebrew
לֵבָב	lay-bawb	3823

Parent Root		
ל	lamed	(staff) In this instance a sense of leading.
ב	bet	(tent) In this instance the person's body.
Picture:		*That which leads or tries to pull the person along in a specific direction.*
Child Root:		
ב	bet	(tent) In this instance the person's body inside.
Picture:	*From within*	
That which controls the person or pulls the person from within		
WHOLE PICTURE:		*The heart is that which leads or gives direction to a person from within (that person)*
Matthew 15: 17-20 "17 Do not ye yet understand, that whatsoever entereth in at the mouth goeth into the belly, and is cast out into the draught? 18 But those things which proceed out of the mouth come forth from the heart; and they defile the man. 19 For out of the heart proceed evil thoughts, murders, adulteries, fornications, thefts, false witness, blasphemies: 20 These are [the things] which defile a man: but to eat with unwashed hands defileth not a man."		

---

[61] There are a few Hebrew root words translated as heart. This one Hebrew word interpretation shows perhaps more clearly, the role the heart plays in a person's life and is close to the description of the heart that Yeshua gave to us.

JUDGMENT	pronounced	Strongs # Hebrew
מִשְׁפָּט	mish-pawt	4941

Parent Root:		
מ	mem	(waters of Life), The waters of life, like blood, living, flowing, also like the waves of the sea in power: chaotic, unstable, massive, or mighty force
שׁ	shin	(two front teeth) Eat, devour, destroy
Picture		In this case, many chaotic issues of life which one considers (chews upon or mediates upon)

Child Root:		
פ	pey	(Mouth), words, communication, scatter, wind, go forth
ט	tet	(snake in a basket) hidden, womb, surround, contain, mad, trap, snare, plot, deceive, lie in wait, etc,
Picture		In this case, speak, state or declare, that which reveals what is hidden, what formerly was not known.

WHOLE PICTURE: In the first part of the word, the parent root, we see many chaotic issues of life, upon which one chews. In modern English, we might say, "someone is mulling, or chewing it over". This means they give it much consideration, much examination. The second part of the word shows speaking, declaring, making a statement, which reveals something hidden. A judgment in this case comes from one mulling over chaotic circumstances, at which point, they speak a final comment which should expose what was not seen before. EG. A person innocent set free, or a person guilty found as such.

LAW	pronounced	Strongs # Hebrew
הרות	Tow-rah	8451

Parent Root:

ת	tov	(crossed sticks) cross, mark, sign, covenant, signature, signal, monument, mark the place, identify, last, last word, etc.
ה	heh	(Man with arms outstretched) Look, behold, wonderful, awesome, God's breath is there, God has done it. Breath, overcome (as in victory after the battle)
Picture		A Covenant attached, or God's covenant with man. Prophetically, the cross and nail shows salvation's plan.

Child Root:

ר	resh	(a head), first, above, highest, supreme, top of, beginning of, top, first position, rule
ה	heh	(Man with arms outstretched) Look, behold, wonderful, awesome, God's breath is there, God has done it. Breath, overcome (as in victory after the battle)
Picture		Above all things and victory. Prophetically, Yeshua, 100% victorious over sin

WHOLE PICTURE: An agreement with God to live above sin. *Exodus 19: 7 And Moses came and called for the elders of the people, and laid before their faces all these words which YeHoVaH commanded him. 8 And all the people answered together, and said, All that YeHoVaH hath spoken we will do. And Moses returned the words of the people unto YeHoVaH. God's instructions for living a holy life.*

COMMENTS: the Jews know the "Torah" as Instructions from God to which they covenanted to obey. Following that line of thinking, if one followed the instructions of God in the Torah, they would keep the covenant. Since they cannot, when they disobey those instructions, these broken instructions show them their need for a Saviour. (Gal 3:24-25 says basically, this same thing.)

LOVE		pronounced	Strongs # Hebrew
אהב		ahava	0157

PARENT ROOT:		
א	aleph	(Ox) strength, strong leader, strongly, with strength, first leader (in the sense of strength), powerful, pulling
ה	heh	(man with arms outstretched) Look, behold, wonderful, awesome, God's breath is there, God has done it. Breath, overcome (as in victory after the battle), can also mean surrender
Picture		The strong leader overcoming
CHILD ROOT:		
ב	bet	(Tent) body, family, house, nation (people) inside, within, etc.
Picture		The house
OVERALL MEANING		In this case, love is a very strong leader that overcomes the house or the person.
COMMENTS		This Hebrew word for love means that 'love', when given leadership, is a strong leader of that person. It is the chief pull in their life. (A person consumed by love in all areas gives love and that love strongly leads the relationship.)

NAME	pronounced	Strongs # Hebrew
שֵׁם	shem	8034

Parent Root:		
שׁ	shin	(two front teeth) Eat, devour, destroy, in this case, tasting.
מ	mem	(waters of Life), The waters of life, like blood, living, flowing, also like the waves of the sea in power: chaotic, unstable, massive, or mighty force
Picture		tasting the issues of life

Child Root: None

WHOLE PICTURE: The word picture shows tasting a person's waters of life. On the surface, that simply does not make any sense, yet in the depth of the word, it does. A person's waters here show their life, their character, *the expression of their being*. When one consumes that, they actually taste the person's life. In other words, they get to know *their essence*. That is not a one time, one moment experience. It normally takes a lifetime to know a person.

COMMENT: A "שֵׁם (shem)" is something that *summarizes the essence or reality of a person*. When KJV interprets that word "שֵׁם (shem)" as name, immediately people associate it with an identity, a way of tagging one person from another. For example, if there are three people in a room, we know the identity of each one by their name. Now, when looking into the biblical meaning of the word "שֵׁם (shem)" we must disassociate ourselves with that thought. We must reconnect it with this one, the "שֵׁם (shem)" summarizes the essence of the person.

PECULIAR TREASURE	pronounced	Strongs # Hebrew
סגלה	seg-ool-law	5459

Parent Root:		
ס	samekh	(hand on staff) grab, protect, support, scepter
ג	gimmel	(foot) walk, stride
Picture		Sceptre and a foot

Child Root:		
ל	lamed	(shepherd's crook) Authority, pull towards,
ה	heh	(man with outstretched arms) Victorious,
Picture		Authority, victory

WHOLE PICTURE: In the parent root, we see a picture of a sceptre and a foot. This suggests walking in authority, in victory, ruling as one goes along. The second part of the word, which we call the child root, shows what comes from walking in victory. First, a shepherd's crook, pulls things into order, and next, from the letter heh, we see God's breath. This summarizes how the victory takes place: by God's Spirit.

COMMENT: Looking at the whole word in the context of the verse, we see that when one puts God first, (obeying His voice and keeping His covenant[62]) they walk as rulers and with the power of His Holy Spirit, they pull things into their proper order, which of course, is God's order. This makes the expansion of the Kingdom of God possible wherever they go, thus they are God's treasures.

---

[62] Under the New Covenant we do this as we live and walk in the power of the Holy Spirit

THRONE		pronounced	Strongs # Hebrew
כסא		kis say	3678

Parent Root:		
כ	kaf	(hand in stop position) Open handed, divine power
ס	samekh	(hand on staff) grab, protect, support, instrument of punishment
Picture		Hand with **unrestrained power**
Child Root:		
א	aleph	(Ox) Strong leader, first leader (in the sense of strength), powerful, (in sense of strong).
Picture		Pulls things with strength

WHOLE PICTURE: Here is a picture of a hand raised, in the same manner as we do today, when we say, "stop". There is also a picture of a sceptre within the pictograph language. Some today might call it a mace.[63] From the Hebrew word picture, we see these two things work together, in a strength that pulls things into order. *A throne is therefore a place where someone strong, someone with unrestrained ability y pulls things into order, their way. In God's case, it is divine authority and divine power.*

---

[63] In Canada and some other countries, without the mace present, governments cannot operate. It is a powerful symbol of authority and the right to govern.

WATCHERS	pronounced	Strongs # Hebrew
רצנ	Naw tsar	5341

Parent Root:		
נ	noon	(seed) life, life that continues on, heirs, inherit
צ	tsade	(a person asleep), (some see this pictures intercession as Ezekiel lay on his side), rest,
Picture		*Inheritance, resting, with the idea of lying in wait and watching*

Child Root:		
ר	resh	(head) first, above, highest, supreme
Picture		*Rule, ruling*

PICTURE: a watcher is one who looks at the *inheritance of actions*, done by individuals or nations, and then, makes a decision, or a ruling, regarding those actions.

COMMENT: This definition fits well with the 2 scriptures in the Word that speak of Watchers. Daniel 4:17 and Jeremiah 4:

SCRIPTURE REFERENCE INDEX

1

1 Corinthians 12: 4-13	74
1 Corinthians 13:4-8	70
1 Corinthians 14:12	74
1 Corinthians 15:40-42	93
1 Corinthians 15:50	90
1 Corinthians 2:12-14	96
1 Corinthians 2:14	31
1 Corinthians 2:16	96
1 Corinthians 2:7-9	109
1 Corinthians 29:10-13	134
1 Corinthians 3:19-4:1	23
1 Corinthians 6:11	91
1 Corinthians 6:9	91
1 John 4:8	71
1 John 5:4-5	166
1 Peter 1:15	133
1 Peter 3:12	108

2

2 Chronicles 16:9	108
2 Corinthians 4:6	81
2 Corinthians 5:17	54
2 Corinthians 5:20	103
2 Peter 1:2-4	137
2 Peter 1:4	55
2 Peter 3:9	157

A

Acts 1:1-3	189
Acts 10:1-11:30	169
Acts 16:6-10	115
Acts 26:15-18	78
Acts 26:18	81
Acts 8:37	167

C

Colossians 1:12-13	67

D

Daniel 2:20-22	55
Daniel 4:17	107
Daniel 6:17-23	117
Deuteronomy 14:2	132
Deuteronomy 28:13, 45	143
Deuteronomy 28:45	147
Deuteronomy 29:29	56

E

Ephesians 1:12-14	92
Ephesians 1:1-4	147
Ephesians 1:15-23	24
Ephesians 1:19-23	97
Ephesians 2:13-14	156
Ephesians 2:15	26
Ephesians 2:1-7	98
Ephesians 6:11-12	116
Ephesians 6:13-18	119
Exodus 18:16	33
Exodus 19:5	132
Ezra 7:25	33

G

Galatians 4:9	188
Galatians 5:19-21	76

Galatians 5:22-23 73
Galatians 6:24-25 72
Genesis 1:1-2 72

H

Habakkuk 2:20 106
Hebrews 1:1-4 104
Hebrews 11:32-40 145
Hebrews 11:6 31
Hebrews 13:8 145
Hebrews 4:2-3 159
Hebrews 6:1-2 188
Hebrews 9:14 72

I

Isaiah 29:13 182
Isaiah 35: 5 81
Isaiah 55:9 95
Isaiah 9:2 81
Isaiah 9:6 144

J

James 1:17-18 53
James 1:22 62
James 4:4 134
Jeremiah 29:13 31
John 1:14 61
John 12:24-25 63
John 14:12 98
John 14:13-17 99
John 14:5-9 104
John 14:6 8
John 16:33 166
John 20:30-31 45
John 3:16 70

John 3:1-7 41
John 5:19 71
John 5:25-29 94
John 5:2-9 186
John 6:18-21 186
John 6:26-27 184

L

Leviticus 11:4 138
Luke 10:27 131
Luke 17:20-21 35
Luke 17:21 100
Luke 24:45 81
Luke 24:49 160
Luke 4:18 77
Luke 8:21 62
Luke 8:9-10 28
Luke 9:12-17 183

M

Mark 1:14-15 43
Mark 12:29-31 45
Mark 12:41-44 182
Mark 3:27 166
Mark 4:11-12 27
Mark 4:13 58
Mark 4:14-20 59
Mark 4:3-9 57
Mathew 25:24 90
Matthew 11:12 28
Matthew 11:5 81
Matthew 14:22-33 185
Matthew 15: 17-20 203
Matthew 16:19 157
Matthew 21:23 69

Matthew 21:28-32 68
Matthew 21:42-44 132
Matthew 21:43................................ 155
Matthew 28:18-20 158
Matthew 3:1-2 35
Matthew 5:3................................ 48, 91
Matthew 5:44.................................. 120
Matthew 6:13.................................. 135
Matthew 6:17-18 181
Matthew 6:19-21 183
Matthew 6:27-34 95
Matthew 7:13-14 89
Matthew 7:21............................. 44, 68

N

Nehemiah 9:5 142

P

Philippians 2:5-11 141
Proverbs 21:22-24 144
Psalm 103:19................................... 107
Psalm 105:40-45 34
Psalm 107:8-20 79
Psalm 138:2..................................... 152
Psalm 139:7-12 116
Psalm 139:7-13 34

Psalm 145:10-13 110
Psalm 146:8 81
Psalm 16:11 105
Psalm 25:12-14 135
Psalm 37:4 138
Psalm 37:9-11 136
Psalm 45:6-7 121
Psalm 47:8 107
Psalm 89:14 122
Psalm 9:7 105

R

Revelation 1:18 161
Revelation 13:7-8............................160
Revelation 3:8 165
Romans 1:20......................................32
Romans 10:13..................................141
Romans 10:8-13 46
Romans 13:1....................................109
Romans 14:17..................................105
Romans 5:12......................................75
Romans 6:3-6 148
Romans 8:2..75
Romans 8:28....................................106
Romans 8:5-9 29
Romans 9:8..92

Cegullah Publishing & Apologetics Academy

(CP & AA)

CONTACT INFORMATION

www.cegullahpublishing.ca

Visit our website for some free downloads to help you live out your Christian life.

www.ingramcontent.com/pod-product-compliance
Lightning Source LLC
Chambersburg PA
CBHW080244170426
43192CB00014BA/2563